My Father's Daughter

by
Jenese Busch

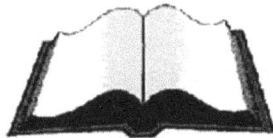

CCB Publishing
British Columbia, Canada

My Father's Daughter

Copyright ©2008 by Jenese Busch
ISBN-13   978-0-9809191-5-8
Second Edition

Library and Archives Canada Cataloguing in Publication

Busch, Jenese, 1929-
My Father's Daughter / written by Jenese Busch. 2nd ed.
ISBN 978-0-9809191-5-8
1. Busch, Jenese, 1929- --Family. 2. Mondschine, Jack David, d. 1974.
3. Fathers and daughters--United States--Biography. 4. Interior decorators--
Illinois--Biography. I. Title.
F586.B88A3 2008   747.092   C2008-902022-7

Publisher: CCB Publishing
British Columbia, Canada
www.ccbpublishing.com

Dedication

To my wonderful family,

Susan "Little Honey"- for your everlasting enthusiasm for life and helping others… for your dedication to your family, your profession and above all to your parents.

Darcy one of the "Darling Doubles"- for your kindness and concern for others. After all the suffering and sadness you have known you continue to strive on and smile. You also share my great passion for all animals and I so love you for that.

Debby one of the "Darling Doubles"- for attempting to help your sister in time of crisis and to endure the pain you are suffering at present. Your love of your devoted husband and wonderful son along with your deep religious conviction shall hopefully be of comfort.

Nancy "Princess Shining Hair" - for always being there for Dad and I, and for the unselfishness you show daily. You are especially thoughtful of us, and show your love in so many ways. Thanks for being my traveling companion and perhaps my best friend.

To our Grandchildren,

Melisa Dawn Marsico - for always being there for Grampa and I and including us in your life. We're so proud of you.

Mathew Raymond Marsico - for your successful achievements in every endeavor you attempt. You should go far in which ever path you choose.

Amanda Michelle Marsico - for your enthusiasm for dance and school. Your generosity to Nana will always be appreciated.

Frankie Laterza - one of Nana's greatest joys as you are always wanting to include us in all of your activities. Great-Grampa would be so proud of your many athletic skills, but most of all of your spirit.

Jackson David Laterza - named for Jack David, for being one of the most loveable little boys I've ever known. I'm proud of your musical achievements and your willingness to play all the "big boy" sports.

Danielle Rae Laterza - For reminding me so much of your Mommy, your sparkling smile, bright inquisitive mind and your spunky spirit. You should succeed in anything you attempt and win the hearts of those around you.

Joseph Jeneson Laterza - now only a baby but with my middle name for which I thank my creative daughter. You should have a wonderful life with such a loving family to support you.

Greggory Nathan Cooper - to a caring loving son who is there to assist his Mother as she needs him. I love your athletic spirit and yet your deep concern for family.

Robbie Lukemeyer - may you continue being the caring, loving person you have always been. Your love of animals is especially gratifying to Nana as well as your deep concern for your Mother.

Heather Lukemeyer - May you experience the true joys of love and home and always realize the great love shown to you by your Mother.

To my wonderful husband, Ray, whose support of all my endeavors over the years has given me the greatest joy of all. You have been there to offer help whenever I was in doubt, and have given me so much love and companionship.

To my Wonderful Mother and Dad,
without whom I never would have written
"My Father's Daughter"

BIRTHDAY GREETINGS
TO MY ·SWEETHEART

BIRTHDAYS ARE DAYS WHEN THOSE WE LOVE
ARE MORE THAN EVER DEAR,
I'M WISHING YOU JUST EVERYTHING
TO BLESS THE COMING YEAR.

Mother & Baby

Acknowledgements

My dear friend and artist - Elaine Moy Hohs
For design of cover

Hilton Head Public Library for assistance on word processor in my
preparation of book.

Perla Frescas for assisting with computer scanning and printing of
documents.

The old trunk I found in a small alcove upstairs and later had it
decorated in a Vintage Design. The contents of which introduced
me to my father and helped me discover my heritage.

Table of Contents

My Father

"A picket frozen on duty
A mother starved for her brood
Socrates drinking the hemlock
And Jesus on the rood
The light from a long dead planet
An early bud bursting the sod
Some call it consecration
And others call it GOD. "
JDM

December 8, 1996

Enshrouded in the mystical awe of the Low Country I begin one of the most important meaningful journeys of my life…an attempt to enter the literary world through the truth of the pen…the fullness of the heart and the somewhat clouded memory of one whose life has taken so many turns, only at last to understand the challenges of past and present.

Filled with the need to leave a legacy to my family I begin the long path and wonder if the triumphs and tragedies spanning over thirteen decades will open hearts of others to likewise share their lives.

Every story has a beginning and ending, an Alpha and Omega with heroes and heroines and mine is no exception other than the hero is extremely unique…my Father, a man of small stature filled with love for all of God's creatures, but leery of mankind, a witty brilliant man who challenged others to their physical and mental strength and always persevered thru determination and conviction and not because of his size nor education. He was a man I really

My Father and his sister facing life's tragedies together.

only understood after his death and yet no greater love have I ever had. The closeness we shared was as close as two humans can be and yet I too had to earn my Father's trust to really know the man, and how can this have taken place when we had so many differing characteristics.

Raised in extreme poverty he learned at a very early age the need for sacrifice, as his Father had been killed, thrown from a horse, leaving his Mother Fannie widowed at a young age with five small children. At the turn of the century life was hard for those without, and this family likewise survived thru love, prayer, and hard work at menial tasks, living from day to day. My Father was only seven selling newspapers on the streets of Duluth, Minnesota and taking home very little to help the family which consisted of Rosalie, his younger sister, baby Gella, and two older sisters, Lottie and Sadie. It seems so strange to write about persons known to you in name only as although we weren't separated by distance, our ethnic backgrounds completely split the family. During the time of his boyhood life there was little time to join in friendship outside the family as need for survival was uppermost and so my Father learned to share his inner thoughts and secrets with his God and all small creatures that he would encounter as a ragged newsboy. For those not knowing Duluth…it's a magical city built upon a hill with terraced streets that lead to the shores of mighty Lake Superior. Approaching the city at night reminds me of a magical place with small stars twinkling above the water as lights reflect from the many levels. The air is crisp and very cold in winter and it is in this setting that I picture my Father with newspapers surrounding his frail small frame under his shabby coat as he attempted to sell newspapers, and so it was on a cold late night that my Father happened to be walking at the wrong place at the wrong time. The next few minutes altered his life forever and have done much to shape my life as well. As he was passing a corner saloon two drunken men loudly cursing and swearing staggered out of the saloon and as my Father huddled in the deep shadows he witnessed one man stab and kill the other. Terrified he ran crying to a nearby church where he encountered a priest who held a Bible, in the dimly lit church, had a seven year old boy place his hand on the Bible and promise God he would "never ever touch liquor," as he told my Father, "it makes sane men go crazy." My Father was true to his word and never in his entire life tasted liquor of any form, but became more aware of deep emotions, somewhat distrustful of his fellowman, and put his trust in God in his 80 some years.

The years that follow are blurred as having never had any contact with any of his family with the exception of Rosalie, his younger sister, years later, I know very little. Much of my Father's life was discovered by me in a small locked trunk after my Father's death and putting together the pieces has been extremely difficult as I loved my Father more than anyone in the world. Thru his actions and thru our many walks holding hands while he told

3

Eau Claire Wisconsin.

that "runneth over" and say to you as we sit here=close each

to the other-You my daughter -have made it "All worth while "- no

shall I ever feel that whatever of little effort I may have put int

this thing called life-has not been fully paid-becase of YOU. .

Love

Love to my darlings-Wards will repair the clock.

My Father's teen years.

4

me stories...stories that were real life experiences put into very wonderful words that I could comprehend, I know my Father was a man of strong conviction. I learned very early that my Father had a wonderful talent for writing, much of which he did as a young man while still living in Duluth. Like many writers my Father took a pen name, his was Jack Demaine, his real name or so I thought was Jack David Mondschine, but either way, he had such deep feelings, was so talented, so witty and loved to converse with anyone on any subject. He would enjoy taking opposing views for the sake of debate and conversation and in most cases was able to win his point. He truly was a brilliant man as I saw him not only with words, but with numbers challenge many a grocery clerk to add the long list of purchases, and while she busily punched in the numbers on an adding machine, my Father would wink, smile and always call out the exact amount and without any hesitation, and always correct in the answer. I marveled at his intelligence and worshipped my Father; and yet underneath was a lonely, often misunderstood man, as he really never had any close friends, only my Mother and myself. The world was his friend, but no one special, animals were all his friends, and that bond was proven to me again and again. To me he was St. Francis of Assisi as he always had time to help an injured or stray animal and taught me to love God's creatures. When I was in grade school it was a common practice for my Father and I to visit the local animal shelter or pound where unwanted or strays were euthanized after their time allotted and so we would drive to the pound in my Father's panel truck, take the poor unwanted stray and drive around the countryside until my Father could convince some kind farmer to give the "poor little fellow a chance." Time and again he would find homes for strays and offered them assistance by taking bags of dog food giving it to the farmer and in most cases when we later checked on the animals they were still where they had been placed or had been given to another caring soul...but at least had been given a chance for life. My Mother did not share in my Father's feeling or his methods of saving the unwanted, but as a child it greatly influenced my life and the lives of some of my family as well.

It was on one of our long walks that my Father recited a long poem to me that seemed to overcome him as tears began to flow. It was the first time I had ever seen my Father cry. He told me that he was going to recite his masterpiece, that he wrote when he was 19 years old as an entry to a contest he saw advertised in a Duluth newspaper…a contest to write something immortal…the reward was not monetary, but rather the work was to be immortalized on a bronze plaque to be placed in a Museum in Istanbul, and so it was he recited for me the words I would see later in a Jewish proverb book written anonymously by a Jewish young man. How could this be as my Father wasn't Jewish…or was he, and if so, why was I never told of my true heritage, only to find all the answers at the age of 40 in a small locked trunk, along with the documentation of his most beautiful work. The proverb is anonymous to the world, but to a loving daughter, and to a curator somewhere in Istanbul there is a name of the author of this beautiful proverb which reads…and ends with "I wept because I had no shoes until I met a man who had no feet." The deepness of such a thought is beyond my imagination and yet it reflects the inner feelings of this wonderful man…who so wanted to share his life and love with me, and yet with my worldly desires and outgoing personality, there was always a barrier for my Father to overcome. Why didn't he share any of these deep thoughts with my Mother?

Gladys Margaret Platte was much younger, 15 years to be exact, a very pretty red-haired girl of 22 when they married. Mother also came from a very poor family with eight brothers and sisters. Likewise my Grandfather on my Mother's side had also been killed at an early age leaving my Grandmother, a young nurse with eight children to raise alone. Times were very difficult and in order to keep the 8 children, my Grandmother put them all in a children's home, only to visit them on week-ends or whenever she

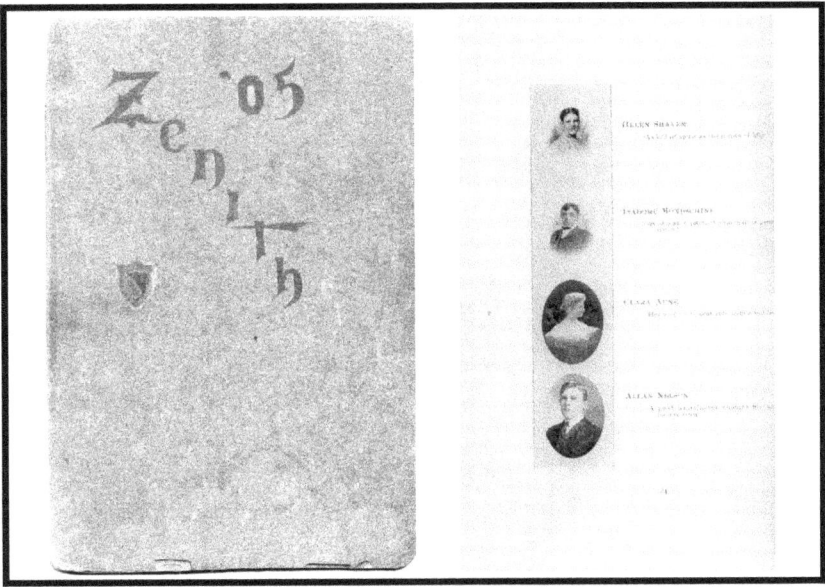

Duluth High School Yearbook

Graduation Class Isadore Mondschine second from top

Duluth High School

could...and so my Mother's entire childhood was spent in a children's home. She was the second youngest and the oldest was Ethel, age 14, who was put in charge of the others. My Mother, Margaret, who later changed her name to Gladys' because the other children called her "Mugsy" which made her cry; Robert, the baby, Orliene, Helen, Alton, Lloyd, Edward, and Ethel Platte were altogether as a little unit among orphans and others much less fortunate. Any toys or treats brought by my Grandmother for her own eight were immediately taken from them and only two could they keep, one for boys to share and one for girls, and so without the love of home, the tenderness of a Mothers and Fathers love, the small children lived until the age of 18 when they were out in the world on their own. The home was extremely strict as to behavior, respect for authoritarian rule, religious training and it also installed a stern sense of morals which carried thru my Mother's entire life as she was timid, avoided discussion thereby never entering into confrontations, modest beyond belief to the point that until the very end of her life I never saw my Mother in less than a full slip. Sex was never discussed and the word alone would have brought punishment. Terrified of strangers, of persons other than those surrounding her such as her own family, she became somewhat introverted and yet had a quiet beauty in her smile, a sad distant look as though she longed for love but was afraid to show her true feelings.

Aunt Ethel, the oldest sibling, was a tyrant according to the other brothers and sisters and since she had been put in charge she took her responsibility to the letter. Her word was law and if the others refused to mind her commands she struck them, often locked them in the basement of the home and on several occasions made them walk thru snow and ice with or without ear-aches, flu, or colds, two miles to Sunday school. Whatever the season they never missed Sunday school or church. It was during their many years at the home that a Scarlet Fever epidemic arose and affected three of Mother's brothers and sisters...Helen, Alton, and Floyd were all left deaf, never to recover. She never forgave my Aunt Ethel and hated her until the day Ethel died. To me, a child, Ethel was a tall strange lady, very eccentric; surrounded by antiques, mostly belonging to my Grandmother. She was married to a very meek man, Uncle Charles who never had anything to say. Ethel was a schoolteacher and devoted her life to teaching. With her tall erect stature, dark hair pulled tight into a bun pinned to her head and small spectacles, she reminded me of a character out of Dickens. Childless herself, she so wanted to be included in the family and since she was shunned by all her brothers and sisters, she turned to her nieces and nephews, so once or twice a year I'd see Aunt Ethel who would always pat me on the head and tell me to stand up straight. How I feared her after all the horror stories told by my Mother and Aunt Orliene and yet this kind lady took in my impoverished Aunt Helen who was deaf and not only took care of her but sent her three children, Douglas, Wallace, and Elva Marie to college. She too had love but was unable to express herself. She had had no childhood and was given an enormous burden of raising 7 children…she remained at the children's home for her brothers and sisters sake long after it was her time to leave because of her responsibility. When Ethel died Charles auctioned all of her belongings, all of my Grandmother's belongings even though each niece and nephew had their names on certain items…mine was a tiffany lamp…and all proceeds were given to "Oral Roberts." He had my Aunt Ethel buried in potters field…an unmarked cemetery for Veterans, where burial is free. This portion of my family history is difficult to accept as no-one with family ties should leave this world alone, but poor dear Ethel did and for this I am very sad. My Mother had no remorse and thought Ethel got what she deserved.

Upon leaving the home my Mother attended Eau Claire State Teacher's College where she got her teaching degree and started her short teaching career in Eleva, tiny town in Wisconsin. A thin tall young women, 5'8" with red hair, light skin, and freckles she began her adult life teaching spelling, penmanship, reading and writing to all grades as it was a country school where all grades were together. The pressure of being in charge after her repressed background was too great and forced her to seek other employment. She answered an ad in the Eau Claire paper for a secretary for the Service Paper Co. and upon going to a poor shabby dimly-lit office...she met a kind, older man with steel gray eyes, wrinkled shirt and a crooked bow-tie...and this small stature of a man of 5'8" was to become a giant in my eyes for he was to be my Father. It didn't happen right away but several months after her employment in the Service Paper Co. she suffered an appendicitis attack and while in the hospital, Jack David Mondschine, her employer visited her with a small nose-gay and told her she needed taking care of for the rest of her life and she so agreed. She was like a frightened little bird and he was the only kindness...the Father figure she never had and so they married.

Within the first two years of their married life, I was brought into the world. My Father had so hoped for a son, to carry on the Mondschine name, a son that could attend the University of Minnesota and become the fine lawyer he had always hoped to become but was never able to achieve. I was to be his male heir and so when a red wrinkled baby girl entered the world on September 3, 1929, the nuns at Sacred Heart Hospital in Eau Claire wanted to know her name, and since no girl's name was ever considered I was Baby A until the day we left the hospital to go home and the nun handed me to my Mother and said, "here is Jenese Dawn, your daughter." The initials JD for Jenese Dawn were the same as for Jack David and my Father had decided that would be my name...and somehow if he wanted a son, he never ever showed it to me as he was more than a giant in my eyes. I totally worshipped my Father and to this day, I thank God for giving me such wonderful parents, even though I truly am my Father's daughter.

My Beginnings

A Daddy's love

A Mommy's love

Life for little Jenese began by moving from the Midwest to Portland, Oregon where my Father took a more lucrative position selling for a large paper company. His job demanded much traveling and this became quite a hardship on the family, as I was frightened of this wonderful man that would only hold me on weekends. Depression was the setting for my early years and although materially we were extremely poor, we were a three-some and my Father would often sing the strains of "My Buddy" which refer to "just Mommy and me and baby makes three" My Mother had never been out of the state of Wisconsin so Oregon was the other side of the world to her and her sight of Mt. Hood from her kitchen window was an impression that left its mark as years later she recalled her wonderful years viewing her beautiful mountain. One of my very first trips was a trip to have a picnic lunch at the foot of the giant beauty, and so after an all day ride in a very old car we pulled over and had out picnic from a view equally as far as from where we had come, and often Mother and Dad would joke about their trip to the mountain…our next trip to a mountain would be many years later. Small pleasures and hearts filled with love were our stronghold as we packed our few belongings and headed back to the mid-west…familiar to both…and really a trip going home. No more would my Father ever leave his little girl for days on end for a bond was forming, never to be broken…not even by death.

Our return to the Midwest was difficult with no job, no home, but with my Grandmother Platte living a short distance from Eau Claire, we lived with her in River Falls, Wisconsin until my Father could establish a home for his little family. Living with my Grandmother was a great source of love as she helped my Mother care for me. I was a rather frail child with large sad eyes that lit up at story time, and always seemed to be questioning and wondering, where is my Father? No one ever told stories like my Father, nor ever cuddled me as close and so the months he was preparing our life in another part of the state seemed endless to a toddler who watched out the window constantly. When the panel truck finally pulled up and we left to go home Mother and Dad said I clapped and sang baby songs all the way to Eau Claire for now we were again a family of three and all together.

Our home was a tiny flat as it was called in Eau Claire, approximately 60 miles from my Grandmothers and as Mother described it as "left over from the depression," but it was clean, had gingham curtains at the window as well as a curtain for the orange crate cupboards that held our dishes and also separated the room into two parts so we could sleep in half and live in the other half. My memory is only recollections of what was told me as the

Mother in River Falls
Grandmother's home

mind of a toddler can absorb only the fundamentals and mine was filled with the love and nurturing I felt in our safe little haven in what was called "God's country."

My Father's job was a salesman for a paper company in Eau Claire, but his territory was only in surrounding rural areas and so he was able to be with us every night and how I waited and watched for him as it meant more stories, more giggles, and more love. What happy times for a little girl whose toys were clothes pin dolls. Mother made them with a pencil drawing on the face and a gingham square pulled over the head to make a dress. I loved my clothes pin dolls. I also had many wonderful paper-dolls that neatly piled in boxes…dolls cut from old magazines Dad would bring home…ones discarded, but to a child, time, dates and fashions are unimportant, but to have an old catalog was a child's dream. What wonderful stories could be created with only a child's imagination and a few clothespins or paper dolls. During the day I also had my many chores, always Mommy's helper and always wearing a gingham apron when I helped, as cleanliness and tidiness were uppermost in our tiny flat.

Always waiting and watching

One day my Father came home to tell us that he at last had a most wonderful surprise for us and his eyes were filled with such pride and accomplishment as we drove up a steep hill on the other side of Eau Claire and pulled up in front of a large yellow frame two story home...a duplex with one apartment downstairs and one upstairs. It was a beautiful home with a front porch and a large yard on a corner and Dad told my Mother he had built "his castle", our home and had been doing this for five years, all the time we were in River Falls and also living in our tiny little flat, and never did he ever let on that he was building this wonderful home...much of it he worked on himself. I remember my Mother crying and saying, "How could you?" She so resented his building her home with no input or suggestions from her. The hurt suffered that day would never be healed, as she continued to hate the home until the day she died, and my Father built more than a home, for now there was also a barrier built around his life, never to be pierced by anyone except me. His dream was shattered and an adult loneliness took over as he and Mother drifted apart. I was so young and loved them both so much, but couldn't comprehend why such a big beautiful home could make two adults so unhappy. My Father would never leave "his castle" and only after his death did my Mother leave it, and to this day I still own my Father's castle...a beautiful home, gracious, simple with windows where I would see my Mother's face watching and always waiting for me to come home or my Father standing on the porch to greet me or to wave good-bye. Several times in the past ten years I have listed the grand old home only to take it back off the market. The area is now a rather low to middle class area and where once stood a lovely old home across the street, there now stands a car-wash, and over the years not only has the yard shrunk to a very small corner lot, but the rooms have become so very small and yet I keep it...this wonderful home with its thick plastered walls, its coal bin and the built in bench and desk in the basement where Dad would sit for hours and write...a desk with a picture hanging over it...a picture of a small yellow home with a big sun, flowers and smoke pouring out of the chimney, drawn by his darling Jenese when she was only five. I may keep the home until I too am no longer here and let my daughters finally make the decision to part with it as I know I never shall as it's like parting with my Father's dream and never can I do that, so I'll continue renting both upstairs and downstairs and hope it will be enough to take care of this lovely old home in the manner that would be approved of by my Father.

Although adult lives were strained in our home, my life continued to flourish thru love of each. My Father always seemed to be finding a way to feather his nest for Mother and I, first by building a filling station next to the home, to bring in extra money. Again Mother cried for weeks on end as she so hated the station and didn't speak to my Father for weeks after he completed the station. He finally after much discourse turned the station into a warehouse for storage, as Mother would not have cars driving in all hours. He then attempted to rent the duplex upstairs only to have the wife...a Mrs. Onstad die and again Mother cried for weeks and so the duplex became a warehouse never to be rented again until after my Father's death.

In the face of all these minor entrepreneurial failures, the station and the duplex rental, my Father lost his job...not because he wasn't the most honest, hard working man, but because of his strong convictions and his promise to a priest when he was seven. He was at a dinner party hosted by the owner of the paper company for all their employees and the owner offered a toast to his wife...when my Father turned his glass over and asked for water instead...he was told if he didn't drink the toast he was insulting the owner's wife and would have to seek employment elsewhere and so my Father came home never to work for anyone else again. He opened what would be the Package Display Company as a manufacturing representative for small sundries such as shoe-laces, razor blades, shaving lotion, hair gel, batteries, pipe cleaners, etc. Our home was to be the office and warehouse for the Package Display Company and so Mother's unhappiness grew to giant proportions but Dad had no place to go. We lived in four rooms, living room, dining room that was used as their bedroom, my tiny bedroom, and kitchen and the balance of the

At home...

home upstairs, downstairs and their original bedroom was a warehouse as was the filling station.

My Father's being home was wonderful to me as now I could see him more often even though he worked very long hours, often coming home 10:00 to 11:00 PM as he sold to grocery stores, small bars, drugstores and drove hundreds of miles in his panel truck working from morning to night. At the end of his day he would go downstairs in the basement, and at his built-in desk he would do his books after fixing his own supper or eating what Mother had left on the table for him. Mother and I always ate punctually at 6:00, but seldom was my Father at home in time to eat with us, when he did come home it was always story time for little Jenese, and after he poured two glasses of milk, one for each of us he'd tell me a wonderful story and tuck me in before sitting down to eat his much delayed evening meal.

How I loved them both and never could understand why they didn't seem to love each other or why Mother cried so often. Each was very lonely and each wanted me to themselves, at least my Mother did. One day she bundled me up and said we were leaving my Father and we went looking for apartments for the two of us. Periodically thru my formative years we would look for an apartment, but never did we leave, and although I was always scared that someday we might…we never did, so I never had to make a choice. The more my Mother took me away, the less money she would receive from my Father for groceries and household expenses. Mother did washing and ironing for others to help ends meet as she was always an "at home mom". What a hard life without material rewards she lived and so did my Father as he worked endlessly, but what about me.

Both saw to my happiness and well-being and so in such a background I grew to love what was important to each…to my Father, the love of nature and wild life, the love of creation and being creative…the ability to accept defeat and find a solution for

Always watching and waiting

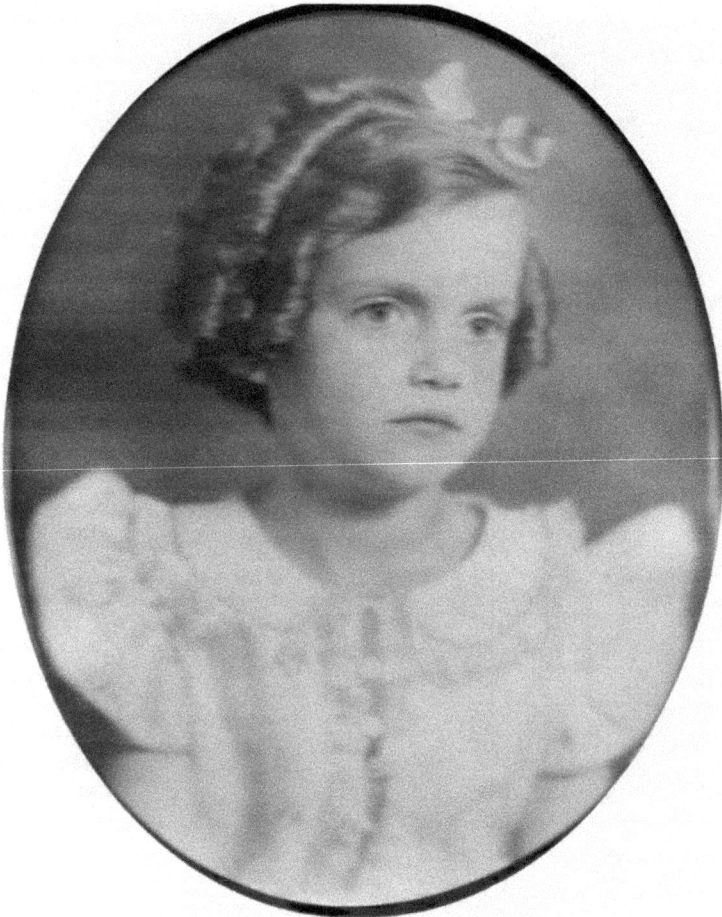

Shirley Temple look at age 6.

any problem and the wonderful ability to communicate with anyone thru reason and expression. From my Mother I gathered the appreciation of each and everything one has, but to always try to do better…to find riches elsewhere and to always seek a better life.

Why a better life…thru the eyes of a child love and understanding is the better life and I had this from both. I especially remember Christmas growing up in that grand old home. Since we had no fireplace we always hung a clothes-line

My first dog...
"Boy," crumpled on highway outside our home in winter... wonderful love

from the front door of the living room to a chair and hung our stockings on this and Santa always came and yet I remember only two presents most vividly…one a sled the Christmas it rained so Dad pulled me around the linoleum floor of the living room and their bedroom. My favorite all time Christmas gift was a beautiful Shirley Temple doll approximately two feet tall with real curls and eyes that opened and closed. She was the most beautiful doll I had ever seen and to this day she has a special place in our home. Christmas was always the same.. .up very early and wearing a clean white handkerchief as a blindfold we'd walk into the living room hand in hand to see Santa's great surprise and he never let down his little Jenese. After opening the gifts and our stockings I would run over to Shermans, a family of three children who lived in the next block. They were poorer than we were as they didn't have indoor plumbing and we did, but how much fun to go over and play with Lois, Marlys, and Dale and to use their little out-house and pump water. Mrs. Sherman was a lovely Norwegian woman from Bergen, Norway who was by Mother's best friend and who in later life became my Godmother when I was baptized. I really don't know why I wasn't baptized as an infant, but because of Rose Sherman I was baptized and attended confirmation at Grace Lutheran church. She was an active Godmother who saw to it that I attended Sunday school with her three and so my Christian upbringing I owe in part to Rose Sherman and yet no one prayed more nor believed in God the Almighty more than my Father. My Mother and Father had no church affiliation and yet they were both religious. Dad attended every activity I was apart of at Grace Lutheran Church and always stood in the back of the church, but never joined the church. Already filled with excitement of activity and friends my parents religious affiliation was of no concern to me and so I never asked but only accepted as the three of us held hands and prayed at home, sometimes the three of us, some times just my Father and I, but never just my Mother and I except on her death-bed.

Our social life was simple as I grew up, as it stemmed around one of my Mother's sisters, Orliene, who lived 10 miles from Eau Claire in the rural community of Mondovi with my Uncle Bill Elkington and their two children, little Orliene (called Sis) and Don, both older than myself Every weekend we'd drive to Mondove late on Saturday afternoon and stay over-night. Mother would bake cookies and pie to take and often chili or baked beans, as my Aunt never cooked anything. The four adults would play poker until the wee hours of the morning and I would have to be entertained by Sis or Don or both. When we were all small that was fun, but since Sis was 6 years older and Don 9 years older it soon became unbearable for them to have me underfoot. I remember on one occasion of telling my Aunt and Uncle that I saw Sis smoking, so of course she was punished. The next time she had to take me along to a party, I was locked in a closet until time to go home, for which again I was able to see that she got her just reward. When I was 10 or 11, they introduced me to the great game of bowling so usually after one, or two games I was ready to go back home and they could then continue on their way without me tagging along. Years later Sis and I became very close. Don became very antagonistic toward me and died never speaking to me after my life was so altered by Father's death.

Our summers always included a short vacation at a cabin near Duluth, Minnesota. The drive was winding and really in the woods. I have no knowledge of how Dad ever found it. But it was on Pequan Lake and the cabin was owned by an Indian. We so loved the pristine water, clean air and the wildlife, which was abundant. I don't think Mother shared our views.

Vacations meant cabins, the lake and nature

Our yearly vacation, cabin at lake near Superior

Reason for living... Love Dad

My school years were all very memorable. Each and every year brought new and exciting moments, and now although I may not remember what I did last week, I remember vividly each and every year. Who could ever forget their Kindergarten...a first time away from home for a whole-half day, and part of that spending on a little rag rug to take the ever so important nap...or the cookie and milk session? I may have accomplished more in my kindergarten class, but I mostly remember eating and sleeping.

First grade was another whole chapter...now full time and being exposed to the meanest teacher in the world..."Miss Sauerkraut", actually her name was Miss Krause, and her nickname was only an indication of a sour face and personality. I really remember little of learning but the joys of pleasing "little Jenese" came in 1st grade as my Father would drive me to the 9th Ward Grade School, approximately one mile...mostly down-hill all the way, and upon arrival at school in my Father's panel truck, I soon became the most popular child in the school for a very good reason. Dad was a great story teller so he'd drive up with chocolate stars and chocolate kisses and would tell stories to the children so I could get the best swing, and have everyone wanting to be around me so they'd get more candy. Seems so innocent looking back, but it was a way to pave the way for success for "Little Punkie" as Dad often called me. What a sweet, wonderful man. The stories were all magical and spontaneous and I so marveled at his ability to capture the small audience or gain attention for one reason or another and somehow it always seemed to work.

Second grade was most memorable as that was my favorite teacher of all...a gentle woman, Mrs. Harper who would often bring her little dog to school and noticing how I responded to her little canine, it seemed fitting that the 1st snow fall and the appearance of a hungry, little stray brought to school by Mrs. Harper that she thought I'd be the choice one to take it home. I remember calling home several times during the day and having Mother say "absolutely not", until finally my Father answered the phone and Jerry became our important member of the Mondschine family home. Mother agreed we'd keep it until Christmas and then give it to my Grandmother, but never was the year of which Christmas was established so we had Jerry for 12 years. My love of animals now firmly embedded, Jerry set the stage for many strays that would cross my path and capture my heart during my life.

My second dog, Jerry

Third grade was a Mrs. Steiner and although I don't recall the academic part of the year, I do remember my excitement at beginning to play the violin with the coaching of Miss Jensen, a music instructor, and the constant practicing that ensued. Practicing was something to look forward to as my parents praised each and every piece starting with a simplified version of Ole' Suzannah. I remember Mother cried when she realized I was playing more than open strings. Spring recital was also a time for showmanship and I was chosen to play the part of a Poppy and was to be all dressed up in red crepe paper. Someone pulled my red crepe paper hat off prior to the performance, but that didn't stop me from performing on stage…the only topless flower, but I learned early to improvise and persevere and so I did.

The mind of a child of nine years old.

Fourth grade was a revelation as I discovered boys…not thru Miss Murphy my teacher, but as a result of Valentines Day. I always gave a Valentine, homemade, to each and every student, but this year I gave two to some of the boys, rather than to share with all the girls. I always received 3 times as many from the boys as I did from the girls but one particular large Valentine with paper dolls inside was my favorite. It came from Larry, a boy rather large for his age, and my hero until the other boys teased him and he no longer spoke to me. Realizing my idol was a sissy who in later years became the town's sheriff, I now threw all my attention to Pinky...my really first crush, and so I now put all claims on Pinky and attempted to sabotage a little girl who also had feelings for Pinky. The mind of a child works in mysterious ways, but I waited for the opportune time and acted promptly, innocent of course, but so planned that to this day it left its impression. I was sent to the school nurse as spots appeared all over my body and I was sent home with the measles. My chief competitor was also sent home for a bad cold, so of course we walked home together, shared a sucker and 7 to 10 days later MaryLou came down with the measles, giving me time to work on Pinky alone. After two weeks of smiles, sparkling eyes and walking me home he forgot all about MaryLou, and all at the age of 9.

In fifth grade my teacher Miss Steiner chose two of her prize students to assist the principal once a week to pass out Goiter tablets, so MaryLou, my famous rival who went on to become the class Valedictorian, and Jenese were chosen...and this task small as it seems now was important to me, as I had been chosen above all others. My need for approval and success, no matter how minute was uppermost in my early years.

Sixth grade was traumatic as Miss Singleton who also was the Music Director didn't particularly like me and on one occasion she had me stand up in front of the entire orchestra for playing out of rhythm with the rest and struck me across the face. I ran out with my violin and cried all the way home. Being an only child of over-indulgent parents, the act of humiliation and violence had to be dealt with and Miss Singleton had a choice to either apologize in front of the entire sixth grade at an assembly or loose her job. She chose to apologize and so I remained in the orchestra where I sat in the first chair never to be bothered again, but in later years I had to defend my daughter in much the way I was defended at the age of 11.

Academics were not a real challenge to me as I managed to get good grades and always was up on all my homework with that willing drive to please.

Seventh grade meant changing schools, area, and meeting a whole new group of students. The 9th Ward school was on the poorer side of town, and all who attended were of the same cultural background, whereas Junior High brought in students from all over the city and soon I was making new friends, still keeping the old, but finding excitement in everything foreign to me. Cheerleading was one of the new extracurricular activities I managed to work into my schedule as well as orchestra where I remained in 1st chair. At the time I didn't realize, but both are somewhat status symbols and so I was indeed popular. Part of the group seemed somewhat snooty to all my former friends, but included me as orchestra and cheerleading put me on that pedestal, and so I now was accepted by the wealthy segment of Eau Claire, the 3rd Warders...It was then that Mother started to work at the factory to bring home extra money. It was time of war and so Mother worked at the US Rubber Company, working shifts and carrying a lunch pail. I remember, I was so proud of her in her navy slacks, white blouse with always a lace hanky in her pocket and wearing a little hair ribbon as she waited for the bus to take her to the factory, but how she hated it. She hated working with vulgar men, hated wearing slacks (pants) as she called them, as she was always such a lady, and she hated her long hours, but she later told me she did so for me, as she was ashamed of our home and now that I was mixing with the upper-class she needed to work to fix the home so I could bring fiends home with me.

A home to remember

How sad...I had never realized our home was anything but wonderful...the bed in the dining rooms, with linoleum on the floors, but soon I realized what she meant. We were poor...and going to the homes of the others living in the 3rd Ward...many with housekeepers and live in maids I started to notice the difference, but decided that if they were friends they liked me for me, and not for what I had. I continued to be as friendly to all...mixed with all, and my popularity only grew. Mother put all of her earnings into our home and soon she convinced Dad to move all his stock out of the 2nd bedroom to the upstairs apartment the basement, and the filling station so she could fix the five rooms in which we lived, and she did.

She painted, stained, bought dining room furniture, new living room furniture which was always covered with the plastic except when someone came and bought area rugs for the living room and dining room, pulling up the cracked linoleum, displaying hardwood floors beneath. The home did take on a new look and I felt we were the wealthiest on the West Side, but really, it was all due to Mother's hard effort to fix it for me.

In the seventh grade I also met some Jewish girls, Charlotte Weinberg, Honey Wenberg and others and we were all friends except my Mother wanted me to become a Job Daughter as my Uncle Bill was a 32nd Mason and could sponsor me. No Jewish girls were allowed in Job's Daughters, but that never affected me, so I became active in Job's Daughters, attending their many dances and parties and always wearing a new dress from one of Eau Claire's finest shops…again paid for by my Mother. It was so important to her that I succeed and rise above our level in life and certainly above her station. She encouraged me to mix with the wealthy, whereas Dad sought the reality…that clothes nor fancy dress did not make the person, nor do fancy homes hard success. My signals were missed, but loving and respecting them both I never questioned, only looked beyond the exterior, while also enjoying my new status in life, mixing with the "upper class."

Seventh grade also became a turning point in my life as my body was no longer that of a young adolescent, but rather one of going thru obvious puberty changes. Nothing was ever discussed in our family as to maturing, sexual changes, or anything beyond the realm of general knowledge and so the day I started to bleed I panicked. I remember going to my seventh grade teacher in a terrified manner as I thought something had happened to me and I was dying. I recall her taking me to the nurse's office where I was given a pad, told this was a normal expectation and it would happen monthly and that I should go home and discuss it with my Mother. To my surprise, my Mother only bought me a box of Kotex a sanitary belt and told me to change frequently and always be clean. When I used the box in 2 days she did tell me that changing didn't mean that often…but that was my total sex education. What I learned beyond was from peers and reading, but never was sex mentioned without a giggle, as it truly was a hush-hush subject in the 40's.

My first real date was with a nerd, Vernon Elbert, who looked like Barney on the Andy Griffith Show, but he was a nice quiet boy and so we went to a mixed dance. My Mother made my dress, a brown & white dotted Swiss dress with a full skirt and I thought I looked beautiful. Needless to say when Vernon told me I looked like Olive Oil I was crushed and realized that skinny doesn't really make it with the opposite sex.

Eighth grade saw more curves in the right places and still the energy level continued, the enthusiasm for the Jr. High Football Team when I gave every jump my all. I also was concert-mistress in the orchestra which I coveted, and so with this background I now faced the big High School and perhaps the best four years of my entire life. Teen years growing up in the 40's were truly awesome, and upbeat. Phrases such as "Hubba Hubba & Jumping Jive" were heard by the bobbie sox crowd with their saddle shoes and school spirit, and I was a always one to be in every possible event and situation. A typical day in the life of a teen is taken direct from my Journal that was part of an English project and assignment by Mr. Hawkinson, better known as "Hawkie", and so to show the lingo and spirit of the time the following is exact pages taken at random from the graded journal. The date was Monday, October 7th, 1947 and the journal reads: "At last my big moment has arrived. I imagine it is easy once you get started, but the question is where to start. After an hour of concentrating I've decided to start at the beginning. Remarkable, isn't it? Oh boy, have I been busy today. It all started in Physics, (the planning that is). It was then that I got the bright idea of chartering a bus to Lacrosse. Without thinking about the cost or work I rushed to the telephone, called Chippewa, and chartered a bus. It was then that I discovered the price, which happened to be a mere $70, but then what's $70 next to seeing our team play? Oh yes, who am I trying to kid. After this I decided it would be nice and necessary to get 34 kids that are reliable, I hope. The next step is to collect the money, not that I'm not a trusting soul, but as they say, "a bird in the hand is worth two in the bush." As up to now I've received $4.00, but I am hoping that tomorrow will be the pay-off, but that remains to be seen.

Tuesday - October 8, What a relief. Here I am with practically all the money and one extra person. Someone is going to have to sit on an aisle seat and oh, do I hope it's comfortable because otherwise I probably will be stiff by the time we get there. More exciting news has reached me today. It was this morning that I learned that I'm dancing with Miss Olson at the Girl Reserve Prom tomorrow night. Boy, is that going to be quite the time. Hubba Hubba!! Wouldn't it be a shame if the band skipped the fourth dance, and my dream of the evening wouldn't come true? Never fear! It was also today that I learned the fate of our Spanish test tomorrow, and of the seven o'clock class in the morning. Our teacher seems to think that our brain is suppose to work better at seven than at eleven, but that I'll have to see. It sure is a cinch that mine couldn't work worse.

Monday - October 14 remember my plans for the football game at Lacrosse. Well, the plans fizzled because the rain drizzled, and when I say drizzled I mean poured. Of all times to start raining it had to start as all of us were waiting for the bus, but even that couldn't stop us. Off we went in the highest of spirits only to get to Whitehall to be told that the game was cancelled. Our spirits fell faster than the rain when we learned that the game was being put off until Monday. Of all days why did it have to be the day school started. Such is life!!

Thursday - October 17…for a year now I have been trying to decide what to do after I graduate. At last I've hit upon one conclusion and that is that I'll never be a cook or have anything to do with cooking. I made up my mind to this after trying to make supper tonight for the first time, alone that is. To start this horrible experience I went to the store only to drive everyone down there insane with questions of what to have and how to fix it. After much thought I decided on hamburgers, potatoes, salad, carrots and pie, which Morn had made this morning. After peeling potatoes and throwing away more than I cooked, I continued to slice an onion and oh what a job. "And my tears flowed like wine."

Jerry given to Jenese in 2ⁿᵈ grade... loving and special

Fun time – graduation party at home, including Jerry

Always in tune

Concert Mistress... beginnings of striving for success.

Teen-age romance...Friends forever

By this time it was quarter to seven and the potatoes hadn't started to boil. Leaving the meat and potatoes for a few minutes I started the salad. As to how it tasted I'll go on to the carrots. These turned out lovely since they were from a can. It was then that I remembered the meat so I started making hamburgers, which really was great fun. After some time the climax arrived and I sat down to eat my well-cooked meal. I never could figure out how the potatoes turned out mashed without any work on my part or how the meat turned out hash, but then miracles do happen.

Wednesday - October 23, Up until now I thought I was a true appreciator of music, but my folks seem to disagree. Today I brought home the most luscious record, "Sherwood Forest", but for some reason or other my Dad doesn't like it any better than my other ones. Gee, I don't believe that songs necessarily have to make sense to be good, such as "Cement Mixer", "House of Blue Lights", "Hey Baba Re-Bop", and others like them. If you're on the beam you naturally appreciate songs like these. I remember when I got a phonograph for my birthday and my Dad brought out some records that he had been saving for twenty years such as "One Alone" & "Girl of my Dreams". In his opinion there aren't songs like that now. I don't believe there is a more beautiful song than "Dream" or "Stardust", but sometimes songs with words get more tiresome than instrumentals such as Woody Hermann's "Northwest Passage" or "Wild Root". Most of us kids agree on that, as you can probably see by looking at some of our collection. Mom doesn't seem to mind them so much and she simply loves "That's what I like about the South". Maybe Dad doesn't like faster pieces but if only slow ones were heard everyday this sure would be a boring place. The radio is playing "Rumors are flying", right now so I believe that I'll sign off until tomorrow, when I can think of something besides music.

Monday - November 18, "Rah-Rah-Rah- at last my big moment is going to come true. Believe it or not we had cheerleading tonight and I'm going to cheer at the game Friday, our first basketball game. Gee, I sure am anxious. At last it will seem as if I belong to the club instead of just warming the chairs every Monday night and yelling my lungs out at the game to help the other cheerleaders along. As yet I don't know if we're going to have a pep assembly, but I sure hope so. Boy the way I'm enthused, we surely should win the game. It's a cinch I'll be yelling for it. I guess our team isn't too hot but I'll write all about that next Friday so tune in then!!

Thursday, November 21, Tonight the string ensemble made their first appearance at our Savior's Church. Boy, was it a mess, our playing that is. We were there around six to eat first. Gee, I never tasted such tuff meat anyway I think it was meat. At last we finished our meal and it was time for us to go upstairs to play. We got up there only to find that we had no music stands and Gale had lost her base music. Serge came to the rescue where the stands were concerned. He obtained some rope and tied something on the backs of chairs to put our music on. Gee, did that look cute. Every time we would turn a page all the music would fall off. We left there around eight only to find that there was a regular blizzard outside. It's only about 5 above zero and by the time we got over town I was practically frozen. But then, after the way we played we don't have to worry about them asking us back for a while.

Friday, November 22, "Boy, today was surely my big day. I cheered at my first big game tonight and I've never been quite so excited in my life. The crowd was huge. They were standing all around. There were six of us, half wore white, and half wore purple. I wanted the purples but ended up with the whites, but then you don't hear me complaining. When at last it was my turn to announce a yell I went flying out on the floor only to have them start playing with me out there. Was I embarrassed and some boys on the sidelines didn't help matters any. Gee, it was fun. After the game, Frye, Pete, J.D. and I went out to get something to eat. Boy did I order because I had been so excited I couldn't eat before the game. After eating all kinds of stuff, I learned that we had to pay for the checks. I nearly ended up with the dishtowel. There was a big dance at the auditorium and did I ever want to go because of being able to wear cheerleading clothes but for some reason or other no one else wanted to so we all went down to J.D.'s house and had a party. Right about now I'm so tired from cheering that I'm going to sign off.

Tuesday - December 3, Rah, Rah, I have to write about it again because it happens so seldom. I'm cheering at the game at Superior

Friday and boy am I glad. This will be the first out-of-town game I've ever cheered at and am I excited. I sure hope we win. We are riding up with Miss Olson. I'm really beginning to like her. It has taken me four years but after so long you rather appreciate her. It's the same with Hawkie. After last year I really am beginning to appreciate you. Boy, I hope I can say that when I get to college and flunk in all my English exams. Anyway you've tried. Say I'm mad at you because I still say my theme wasn't late and you insist that it was. If I had time I'd prove it to you but then you probably wouldn't believe it. I sure hope that doesn't count a lot on our marks. All in all I'm beginning to like all my teachers. I can't figure out what is coming over me.

Wednesday, December 18, Tonight was our "Pop Concert". Yesterday afternoon we had one for the students and tonight it was for the adults. It sure went off swell. I wore my pink formal with a hoop skirt and I had half the band wondering if I did have a hoop on or not. We started out by playing "Intermetzo", then "Liebisfried", then "Gesu Bambino", and then our soloist Bryon Heeley sang two Christmas songs. It has never failed. Every "Pop Concert" the singer always stands on my formal and sure enough he did it again tonight. The orchestra's last piece was the "Desert Song" which is a beautiful number. When it came time for my solo "One Alone", I was very calm until I stood up and there in the front row sat the boys yelling at me. Really down deep they were more scared for me than I was myself. The boy with the spot light was a little late but otherwise it went over pretty good, anyway I received a lot of compliments. Just call Fritz Kreissler and I'll give my autograph.

The Journal continues on and on showing a typical teen of the 40's filled with all the emotion one could possibly imagine from a starry eyed girl, now dating one of the richest in Eau Claire a handsome young man...one year older than myself and from the 3rd Ward. He'd pick me up in one of his Father's new Cadillac's and we'd cruise the streets and my popularity was skyrocketing. I was no longer the skinny little girl from the other side of the tracks but perhaps one on the most popular in ECHS and I never let my position change me as I loved everyone and enemies I had none.

During these four years, I took Mother and Dad for granted. Dad was at every one of the High School games to cheer for "his punky"...no matter if blizzard or rain, he was a loyal fan of the "Old Abes", but it really wasn't the team, but his princess that he was cheering for. Mother seldom attended as working in a factory all day took its toll and so I continued reaping all the love and worldly possessions that parents would shower on me. I always had the best clothes...Mother saw to that...and Dad kept everyone tuned in to watch for that "darling" on the field or stage, as "she's special". Even my violin lessons must have been a tremendous sacrifice, but nothing was too good for Jenese.

I did start to have friends to our home...and often two or three fellows would come up to see me and end up talking to Dad on sports for hours, while I'd be out with someone else. Dad could charm honey from a bee, and his mastery of the English language was unparalleled. He loved to converse, and seldom had any communication with Mother as she was either too tired or wasn't interested in what he had to say...so to have a captive audience of teens, especially males, was Dad's great delight. He encouraged me to always invite all the fellows up and for my 17th birthday he surprised me with a party of eight fellows...all dates, or previous dates that came up for cake, ice cream and conversation with Dad because I had other plans for late evening with Jim Nagel...my true love. Jim and I dated for three years and although I really thought he would be my life long companion my Father saw this as only a teen infatuation that would end with college, and so it did. He was the son of the owner of Caterpillar Tractor...a wealthy non-ambitious, likeable boy, but as Dad often said, "he's nothing but a rich man's son," and such words of wisdom. Mother adored Jim as he offered prestige and money for Jenese, but luckily I listened to my Father, for Jim took to drinking and in later life died after going thru his Father's fortune...and yet I shall always have a weak spot in my heart form my first true love, Jim. He always respected me and although we had many opportunities, never did we engage in anything more than tender petting. Years later, he told me he wishes he had made me pregnant so I would have married him.

Both parents continued to offer me there all...Dad the wisdom and insight into the great beyond, the trust in God Almighty, and the worth of man by "sweat of brow" as he would put it. Mother continued with her doting on her only child...to offer me the best she could buy. I'll never forget my Senior Prom when Mother and I went shopping for my formal. The Fashion Store was Eau Claire's finest and there I found a beautiful pink off the shoulder gown with a full tiered skirt and black satin bows adorning the gown. We were standing with the clerk looking at the $250.00 price tag when one of Eau Claire's richest arrived with her daughter Bobette. The Mother made the statement that they would take the dress Jenese had on as no way could she afford it...at which time Mother said, "We'll take it!" I don't know how many hours Mother stood on her feet at the factory to pay for that dress, but I remember her pride in seeing me look as she had always wanted the best for me.

On My Own

Early teaching... be yourself at Sorority Rush

C

Omega

of Delta Gamma

Requests the Pleasure of Your Company for

TEA

on *Saturday, September 18th*

from *4:00* to *6:00* o'clock.

Please respond to

Virginia Campbell
103 Langdon St.
Madison, Wis.

THE UNIVERSITY OF WISCONSIN 352
PERMIT TO REGISTER WITH ADVANCED STANDING

Your credentials have been approved for admission to the College of Letters and Science . You are entitled to register with approximately 30 credits of advanced standing toward the degree of Bachelor of Science (Hygiene)

OFFICE OF ADMISSIONS (ADVANCED STANDING)

Date July 15, 1948 By: ea

(Registration directions—see reverse side)

Miss Jenese Dawn Mondschine
946 Third Street
Eau Claire, Wisconsin

(Valid only for the 1st semester 1948–49)

$346.00   Sept 3 1948 No 2873

RECEIVED OF Jenese Mondschine

Three hundred forty-six and 00/100 DOLLARS

Registration fees & Board Summery Hill
Academic Year 1948–49

By William Mc?

College was a chapter of its own for trials, triumphs, and tribulations all were they're starting with excitement of choosing the right college. Although Dad had always been loyal to the University of Minnesota and he and I looked at the Campus together, he wasn't surprised when I chose the University of Wisconsin in Madison. He went to both with me to look them over, and again Mother was unable to go. Maybe the thought of her one and only leaving was too much to face, but the day did come when I left for the university of Wisconsin...one of the big 10's with 25,000 students...me coming from a small mid-west town, and never having been away from home for more than an occasional slumber party, or for a week at my aunt's cottage with my friends. I was now entering into the adult world and all my teaching; moral, ethical and philosophical would be challenged. Walking into my room was eye opening to be sure, as my roommate was draped on the bed, scantily dressed, smoking and talking on the phone. She was fresh from a girl's school, came from a wealthy family, and was truly a worldly figure. My Father was appalled and attempted to get me moved to another room at Ann Emery or to another dorm, only to be told that they would look into it. After several hugs, kisses and tears, I watched Mother and Dad drive slowly away and it seemed for the first time that my life was over...how I wanted to run after that wonderful old paneled car and go back to my childhood where I felt warm, safe and loved, but as Dad had always told me, "Jenese Darling, we're tuffies, you and I and we can always be strong and face whatever life gives us. Remember God Almighty and trust your better judgment and instincts" and so I re-entered the dorm and began my life on my own.

Dealing with Mary, my rather phony roommate, turned out to be short-lived as she soon became pregnant and had to leave school. Her replacement roommate was a senior who decided to have her father pay for her diploma and sleep her days away, missing most of her classes. I'll never know how she graduated, but she did and again I saw what money and donations can do.

College meant party time, philosophy soon changed

As for me, I had found my niche. I had gone to the Sorority Rush all alone, rather scared and wearing all black as I had heard that black was proper for such an event. Mother and I had attended a Tearoom luncheon at Dayton's where the narrator advised what to wear for Sorority rush when attending college. Obviously Dayton's in Minneapolis wasn't aware of what was happening in Madison, Wisconsin, as I looked ridiculous in all black, hat and gloves included. The only accessory that wasn't black was a long strand of pearls twice wrapped and knotted. After visiting the first Sorority House and having a miserable time, I went back to the dorm, shed my hat and gloves and went to the other Sorority Houses determined to try to win them over. I know that I had to make an impression and so I told them each the same story of my dilemma on registration day. All the Frosh met in the Bascom Hall where registration packets were given out as names were called. When the spokesperson got to the M's there was a big delay and then over the intercom came the statement, "Will Jenessee Moonshine please step forward. Everyone laughed and looked around. About ½ hour later I went up and whispered that I was the "Jenessee Moonshine they were looking for." I remembered how Dad told his many stories and so the "Moonshine story" was my entry into Sorority life as I got callbacks to all the Sororities except the first where I wasn't myself. In open rush it's very difficult to be chosen if you're not a legacy or sponsored by someone, so for a young girl from a small town to get into one of the top Sororities in the Country, Delta Gamma, it was a real feather in my cap.

Naturally sorority dues and expenses were substantial, but Mother never complained, only paid all the Sorority statements. Dad paid tuition, room and board, but Mother's efforts paid the extravagances beyond. I had worked the summer between high school and college as a nurse's aid at the local hospital, but had spent all that I had earned on clothes for college. I decided that I really should help with my expenses so I decided to get a job.

I was eighteen when I entered the entrepreneurial world by answering an ad for a "sales clerk" in the window of the "Greasy Spoon Restaurant." Upon entering the paper-draped windowed

Dating a "man" – Chet and I

establishment I was met by three college law-students. They were
wealthy Jewish young men that had been set up in business by
their respective Father's to see what they might do with a business.

They told me their plans to open an exclusive college boutique for both males and females, selling only the best in clothes...cashmeres, camel coats etc. After a short interview they offered me the job, which included hiring others, planning and executing weekly fashion show. I was so excited as now I not only had a tremendous job, but one that would give me the popularity and exposure on Campus as well.

The shop was called "Bruce & Co." and it was nothing less that totally successful from the start. These three young men knew how to market merchandise and make money. I soon became one of the best dressed on campus as I had ever color cashmere available and there was no stopping the direction they were going. I organized, interviewed perspective models from each Sorority and once a week I had a narrated show at a different Sorority House offering only discounts on the clothes worn to each models, and all wanted to model and all bought their clothes. I made *$25.00* per show and I gave my roommate *$5.00* per show for playing background music on the piano. When I wasn't at a Sorority House I was at a Woman's dorm and my popularity mounted as did my ability to handle a microphone without any script cards as I knew my subject, clothes, and so I just described what I saw. The only problem with all the time spent being the best dressed or most popular was the toll it was taking on my studies. Soon the first Semester was over and I was called into the Counselor's office for freshmen students as my grades were all below standard and it was then that I had to tell a real white lie, both to the University and to my parents, "that I was still adjusting to being away from home for the first time, but that I was getting better" which kept me in college...on probation...but none the less still a student, but now I had to study as the realization that study was my number one commitment took over and soon I was able to establish study habits that would permit me to continue on in somewhat an adjusted manner. I was able to continue on in the world of fashion, sorority life, dating and all the fun activities without any major

1950 " *U* " *of Wisconsin Prom Queen*

problems. By the time I had finished my freshman year I had been nominated for Military Ball...had weekly fashion shows and was super active in Delta Gamma, and was maintaining and A-B average, with an occasional C in Sciences.

Chet came into the picture my sophomore year. After Nagle and high school there were many, many dates, some strictly plutonic, and I never missed a fraternity dance or party, didn't smoke, drink more that 2% beer or engage in any more than a good night kiss. Chet was different. I was 19, he was 25, an Ex-Marine, Polish and was working his way thru college as well as helping to support a younger brother. He was tall, rather handsome, and into physical fitness as an Ex-marine. I had never dated a man before and it really was an infatuation, or possibly my second love. Up until now there was no one for my folks to meet as everyone else was a party-date only, but Chet was different. He was a member of the Chi Phi Fraternity, and after only one month of constant dating he professed his love for me and gave me his fraternity pin to wear and show we were going steady. He spoke of marriage and I wasn't ready for either. We literally discussed sex, and I found I not only was totally embarrassed, but not certain what to do. Thank goodness he respected my morals and never tied to take advantage of me as I wasn't ready for such a commitment and was totally naïve.

The year was 1950 and Chet's fraternity the Chi Phi's nominated me for Prom Queen. At the University of Wisconsin the Queen is elected by an all campus election and her date automatically becomes Prom King. There were about 60 candidates early on, but after elimination it came down to the final 12 who all had to campaign for the coveted trophy. I remembered my popularity in high school and how I succeeded by befriending all and not staying in my own little click, as did most of the contestants. There were no Jewish candidates among the top 12, so I campaigned at all the Jewish sororities and Jewish fraternities. I

Graduation with new last name and new look

also campaigned at all the independent dorms and houses for both men and women as no independents were in the final. The results paid off and when the all campus election took place there were no only 6 contestants, 5 would be on the court and one would be Queen, the results announced at the Prom to be held in the Grand Ball Room at the Student Union, the grand ball room was an impressive room with magnificent marble columns. The staging was all the glitter and glamour of movies of the 50's, the orchestra Ralph Marterie, and the theme, "The Continental." Mother, of course worked extra hours to buy me the most beautiful gown I had ever seen...white strapless tulle covered with silver glitter, full skirted to emphasize my 23" waist. I wore my hair very long and had a single gardenia in my hair. Mother and Dad were there as were hundreds. Chet wore a white dinner jacket and was so tan and handsome. We must have made a truly dashing couple. I had campaigned with vigor until days before the prom, and now it was up to all that attended as each was given one ballot. We rehearsed the scene...the winner would step thru a sparkling globe onto the stage and down the steps to dance the first dance with her King. I remember waiting breathlessly, hoping against all hope, when they announced me the winner. All cleared the floor for me to dance my favorite dance. I turned and asked Chet if he minded if I danced it with my Father. Soon Dad and I were the only two on the dance floor with the spotlight on us while Ralph Marterie played my favorite "Some Enchanted Evening". I recall Dad saying he had never danced before, but we didn't dance, we literally floated over the dance floor and I'll never forget the tears of pride in his eyes, and I knew then that I was truly, "My Fathers Daughter". This would be pointed out to me many times throughout the years.

Mother too was thrilled even though she hated Chet. She was appalled that after years of work and sacrifice I should fall for a "poor Pollock", and she hated him without even knowing him. Dad in turn suggested we ask Chet to join us on a trip to Niagara Falls where the four of us would drive both ways for one week or so. Mother didn't like the idea and hardly spoke the entire trip, only enough to point out his shortcomings to me. By the end of the trip I gave back the pin and decided to date others as well. Chet and I dated occasionally as he had graduated and would come to Madison as often as he could to surprise me, but I was always out with someone else. On one occasion he appeared with an engagement ring and said he wouldn't share me anymore and became very strange. I remember jumping out of the parked car and running and hiding in the dark while he searched for me in vain. Never before had I been so terrified, but something told me to run and hide. How I got back to the dorm that night I'll never know, as it was past curfew, and I had walked for hours. I was sobbing, but unharmed, and I learned never to put myself in harms way again. I never dated Chet again as his anger had scared me, but years later we rekindled an adult friendship.

All during my sophomore and junior years while dating Chet, and after breaking it off, I kept seeing a most handsome fellow driving in a new convertible around campus. He would smile and wave and I would reciprocate wondering who was this handsome gorgeous man and where did he come from. As was customary among the female coeds, when one received a call from an unknown the badger yearbook was quickly checked for a look-see. During the one and a half year time frame I would get a call from the same individual, a Robert Farrel, I would check, double check and have my roommate check for a face in the Badger, but to no avail, and so I never responded with any encouragement via phone, but when I would see the stranger, the flirtation would continue, but never did I ever connect the two happenstance's. I was now a student nurse and living at the nurse's dorm when again Robert Farrel attempted via phone to make a date and so in order to rid this pest from my phone line forever, I made a 15 minute date, to be after I finished the 11:00 p.m. shift on duty. I thought that after a short cup of coffee I could end the relationship once and for all, but never have I been so shocked as when I walked into the small coffee shop to see the same handsome "Mr. Wonderful" that I had been encouraging for so long. It was truly love at first sight and how vividly I remember stating to my roommate on my return that I had met the man I was going to marry. Looking back it was totally an infatuation and a "love is blind" situation, however in four short months I eloped with a total stranger. All along the way he had shown me so many red flags, but I never saw anything but him. Perhaps it was his eyes...never before had I seen such eyes, soft brown like those of a deer and a sadness and innocence in his eyes that a definite power over me. His sandy blonde hair slightly waved, his tanned skin and a smile that would cause any female to melt was all that I saw. So very handsome and yet a definite loner...never surrounded by friends or acquaintances, but always alone, as if removed from all those around him. On one of our first real dates he told me that he had loved me for over two years and seeing me on campus returning his overtures was confusing to him. I sheepishly told him of checking the ever-faithful yearbook, which managed to keep us apart so long.

Bob told me that older persons while living in Boston adopted him as an infant. His parents had been killed in a car crash and he was left an orphan at the age of 9 months so the Farrels had adopted him and I could never figure out why he was so filled with anger and hate for his adoptive parents, especially after meeting them. The first encounter with his parents was a skating rink where Bob and I were ice skating when a large luxury auto drove up and I was introduced to Marion, later called "Mama Liz" and David Farrel. They seemed to be genuine, loving, doting parents who worshipped their only child, Bob. They extended a dinner invitation for me to come to their home, which was unlike my home environment. They lived in Maple Bluff, near the Governor's mansion, in a charming home filled with antiques and beautiful artwork. A huge life-size portrait of Bob at the age of five hung over a marble mantel and everywhere I looked was a reminder of their son. The evening went much too quickly and I couldn't imagine why would anyone hate two such lovely people.

The holidays were approaching and I was going to Eau Claire for the break, but Bob convinced me to come back early to spend New Year's Eve with him as he had planned a large New Year's Eve party at his home...about 25-30 couples. I had so much to tell Mother and Dad when I arrived in Eau Claire, about this very handsome, rich young man that I was totally in love, and wanted them to meet him. Mother's approval was immediate, based on only what she heard, but Dad reserved any comment until after he had a chance to know this Bob Farrel. What did he do? What were his goals, his plans for the future, his outlook on life, his feelings about children? None of these questions had even entered my mind. I only knew I was in love so expected them to love him too, as they had always tried to please Jenese before. The meeting between my parents and Bob was to be in Minneapolis for the Wisconsin vs. Minnesota football game, which was to be held after classes resumed from Christmas break. Before the meeting there was first New Year's Eve and the planned party at Bob's home. As usual Mother and I went shopping for the something special to wear. So with sadden hearts, Mother and Dad put me on the train headed for Madison.

New Year's Eve was a complete disaster as no one showed up for the party. Catered food was abundant, and the home beautifully decorated for the event, but no guests, only me. It was on such a night and in the midst of confusion that Bob presented me with a diamond, but told me not to show his parents or wear it around them, as he was to marry a Vassar or Wellsley girl and I didn't fit the picture socially, so would never be accepted. Excited and yet confused I kept our little secret around his parents, but not mine. I had to call and tell them the great news immediately and the reaction was as before with only one parent rejoicing.

The meeting day occurred and I waited with Mother and Dad at the Minnesota stadium entrance for Bob to appear. He was rather late, but made his polite apologies and the four of us headed into the bleachers. I don't know who won that day or what even happened as I was on "cloud 9" as was Mother; however Dad spent most of his time attempting to get to know his future son in law. From Minneapolis it was a short drive to Eau Claire where he was to stay overnight at our home. Since our home had but two bedrooms, Mother had made a reservation for him at the Eau Claire Hotel, the finest in Eau Claire. He appeared rather hi-brow and not too interested in our home and family and acted strange the entire time, but once we left to drive back to Madison he changed back to the Bob I loved. On our trip back to Madison he told me the only way we could marry was to elope as his parents would never approve of me or of my background, as we were poor and Mother was a factory worker whereas his parents were wealthy and socialites.

I agreed to his plans, but told him I had to tell my parents. I could never elope without telling them first, so I made arrangements to go home the next weekend and tell Mother and Dad of my plans. Looking back the irony of it all becomes too much. How could I have hurt the two dearest persons in all the world to go off with an unknown, and so the future was being shaped without rhyme or reason, but on the foolish whim of an impetuous young girl with everything to loose and nothing to gain, but I never saw it that way.

My evening with Mother and Dad was one to remember. Mother cried tears of joy and agreed that we could never have the type of wedding needed for such persons in the social set of Madison, and yes he was nothing less than perfect. After her excitement and kisses she went to bed and Dad and I remained quietly talking, crying and facing the tragic decision together. He was totally unimpressed with Bob and pointed out a flaw that I hadn't noticed...that of eye contact. He had never had eye contact with Dad during their conversations and this bothered Dad as honesty, integrity, and eye contact are all connected. I listened, heard every word, and yet my mind was made up. By early dawn Dad held my hand and told me that I was of age and he couldn't nor would he attempt to stop me, but told me to "remember the door to our home always swings in, my Darling". With that and a heavy heart I left, telling them that I'd call them and let them know where and when, yet asking for their secrecy as to our plans and intent. Never would they betray their only daughter nor did they.

We set the date for May 10th, 1952 and with my roommate Jan, drove to Dubuque, Iowa to have the Justice of the Peace perform the ceremony. From there we drove back to Madison, dropped Jan off at the nurses dorm and went to have our wedding pictures taken by DeLong Studio which Bob had arranged for. The irony is that DeLong was a personal friend of the Farrel's, so news spread quickly. After a brief sitting, me in a white Hammacher suit and small white hat. We left for a two-day honeymoon before I would begin my summer session at the University of Chicago in

Obstetrics in the School of Nursing.

The first call was to Mother and Dad who were anxiously awaiting the call...tears of joy and sadness pursued and then I was introduced to the ugly side of life, as the phone rang every 15 minutes with screaming, accusations, threats, talks of annulment, etc, as Farrel's had just heard. Our entire weekend was a disaster and although I looked to Bob for support and tenderness, there was none. He was impatient, angry and not the man I thought I had married. Sex was painful and scary as I had not been prepared for any part of it. Thank goodness Bob used condoms, as I had nothing. By the time Monday arrived and I was dropped off at the nurses' dorm with a brief goodbye kiss, I wanted to run home, back to my safe haven but I knew I had made the decision on my own and had to live with it. The summer held no surprises...I wrote daily to Bob but he never answered. He would call occasionally to tell me about this or that golf tournament that he had entered. He seemed to play golf daily and I had no idea of any job or support means on his part. Confused, hurt and alone I attended classes, clinic at Chicago lying-in and back to the dormitory as the weeks passed. By late July I had gone nowhere, seen no one, but only sat crying in my room after classes ended. On one such day the other student nurses encouraged me to go across the street from our dorm to Stag Field and watch the fraternities play baseball. Washing away the tears I put on some shorts and headed for Stag Field where fate took a hand. I was standing very near the 3rd base bag when the umpire called out to a tall rather upset fraternity man. He accused me of causing the out...everyone laughed and decided since the game was over it was time to go out for sodas and celebrate. When you're in college you celebrate win or loose. Everyone agreed and as I turned to go back to the dorm, the tall ball player that I had upset earlier asked, "Aren't you coming?" I responded by saying that I couldn't because I was married and to this he just laughed and reminded me that was only a group soda. The group soda turned into group parties...fraternity parties at the

Psi U house, walks on the beach...talks while sitting on the rocks over looking Lake Michigan, and although I wasn't in love with Ray, the fellows name in question, I knew I had made a drastic mistake by eloping. Ray was kind, quiet, deep thinking, caring, honest, and religious...all the things I admired. His looks unlike Bob's were clean cut, nice, but not handsome. He wore glasses, understated in his dress and manner, but was always surrounded by friends, and from all appearances it seemed like everyone liked Ray. There was nothing not to like. On one occasion, he asked me to a Sunday dinner at his parent's home in Skokie, a nice large home on a quiet street with nice parents, very religious. His Mother spent most of her time in the Baptist Church...his Father was in the wholesale meat business. It was a nice afternoon and I appreciated a real home cooked meal after student nurses' dorm food. I was starting to enjoy life again and feel like the co-ed Jenese...last years Prom Queen...fun and free, but soon it had to end as summer was coming to a close and I had to return to classes at the University of Wisconsin and to married life. Watching Ray study for his law school exams was very difficult, as I knew I had passed up my chances of ever meeting a Ray, a descent loving man. On our last time together Ray gave me a lovely sweater as a remembrance of our brief encounter, good friends...with never so much as a hug. As ethics would have it I had to refuse his generous gift and we parted...never to see each other again and I went back to Madison. Bob picked me up and talked of nothing but trophies, tournaments and excuses for not writing nor coming to see me, but then it was only for four months. He did have the master plan at work and his parents were willing to see me with open arms.

Upon our arrival we went to a hotel and called them rather than go to their home. His Mother screamed in the phone...called me a whore and hung up. Soon his Father called back and said he was coming over to the hotel to see us, without her, as "Mama Liz" was sick. David Farrel was a gem and I really learned to love that dear man as years went on. He put us up at the hotel...paid all expenses until something could be worked out. He had also lined up a job for Bob with Household Finance Company in Madison, so I now went back to classes, Bob went to work and we stayed at the hotel for a short time. After three to four weeks there was a telephone call from Mama Liz stating that she had a surprise for us. The surprise was a beautiful apartment near campus overlooking Lake Mendota with all new furniture, which had been designed by a decorator including even the dishes. I walked into a Showcase apartment, all done, as she would want for her son to live. Some might have resented her taking over completely, but I was overwhelmed and very grateful. I had no knowledge of design and no flair for decorating, so this was a dream come true. Bob seemed unimpressed and acted as though he expected nothing less. I did have rules and regulations set down by Mama Liz, the apartment had to be clean, tidy and perfect at all times and always before I left for 7:00 am class I had to rake the shag rug, a 10 x 12 in the living room. The apartment was one large room with a kitchenette...a plaid sleeper sofa doubled as our bed and a chest was in a large closet. Mama Liz had organized everything for me and almost daily I would come home from classes and she had been at "her doll house", playing bridge with her friends or possibly she just brought over the evening meal. I do think the initial acceptance and the apartment was David Farrel's idea, but nonetheless, the more appreciation I showed, the more they showered attention and gifts on us. We were only in our apartment for four months when Bob got a notice that he had to report for basic training so we had to move. I was to live with the Farrel's until he got his orders where he was to be stationed.

Moving day was traumatic as Bob at the last moment had a weekend retreat for ROTC, and so the three of us along with a small moving company proceeded to pack and move to the Farrel's where I would live while he was in basic training. We later found out there was no ROTC retreat and he had just chosen not to assist with the move at all - a blatant lie which later illustrated a habitual pattern in his personality and a flaw realized and accepted by his parents, but completely foreign to me as I had always been taught - "It is better to play fair and loose than to cheat and win", again wonderful words of wisdom taught to me by my Father at a very early age never to be ever forgotten.

I did live with the Farrels for the four months while Bob was in basic training and became very close to these two wonderful people. During that time David Farrel always drove me to the University to attend all my nursing classes and was there to take me home where we'd have a wonderful dinner together and have an hour or so of cards before studying and to bed. On days when there were no classes, Mama Liz would take me to Antique Shows or shopping for fine accessories or furnishings or we'd visit the home of the Oscar Meyer family or Governors Mansion where I always managed to use proper manners and yet add spark to the conversation. Although I felt a closeness to the Farrels, I so regretted with sadness that the parents would never blend or mix but my love and loyalties were always with my Mother and Father. I could not or would not become any other person then their own beloved daughter, so my life now had two distinct paths. During the time with the Farrels I was in constant touch with Mother and Dad and did go to Eau Claire to visit them but after the one encounter they had with the Farrels, they never saw each other again. This was before Bob left for boot camp when the Farrels invited Mother and Dad to their home for a Sunday dinner. They arrived in their best - Mother wore a new dress and was extremely nervous while Dad wore the one sport coat he owned and was himself, not looking at the material wealth, but attempting to see his new son-in-law and his family what their role would be in his daughter's life. The afternoon was uncomfortable at its best and Mama Liz had a way of looking down at my parents, which angered and upset me, while my Father sized them up with a clear unblurred vision. Bob was rude and oblivious to both sides and I felt like a referee being torn apart. When I walked Mother and Dad

Sharing Pixie and nature

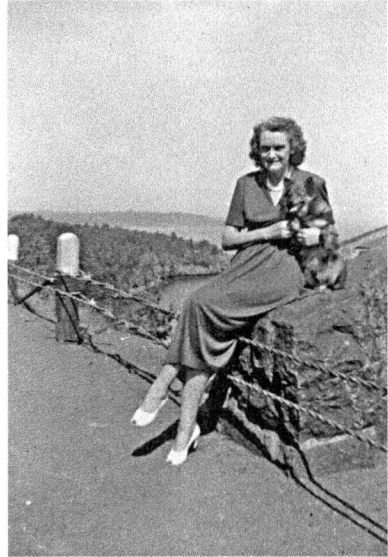

Sharing Pixie and nature on shores of Lake Superior

to his old van I could see the hurt in their faces and yet Mother said she was so happy for me that I had married so well, but my Father only kissed me and told me how proud he was of his "darling daughter" and to remind me that we were "tuffies" and that the "door always swings in" and so they drove away. I realized he knew that life was going to be a real challenge with Bob, but that I should know he was only a phone call away.

Upon arriving home the large yellow home seemed very empty, so Mother and Dad decided they needed another dog. Mother wanted a small dog. Dad just wanted any dog to love. But he did give into Mother and they purchased the only pure breed they ever owned, a Pomeranian, named Pixie.

After he finished his boot camp I took the train to Jacksonville where Bob met me and we first looked for a car we could afford. His Father had given him money to tie us over until we were settled, so we chose to live in Jacksonville Beach, about 20 miles from Jacksonville where I worked as a graduate nurse. Bob was at the base most of the time...got night shifts often, so I was usually alone and drove back and forth between Jacksonville and the beach. We purchased a large old Hudson with a chrome duck on the front, as I needed transportation for work. On one occasion it was no doubt the size and weight of this old car that saved my life as I was at work when hurricane warnings were posted. I was about to make the drive to the beach and heeding no warnings from others. I was the only one on A1A Highway with 75 mile per hour winds, but through sheer determination and luck I managed to get to our little apartment where I watched the waves crash over the boardwalk, thinking it was the most awesome sight I had ever seen.

From Florida we went to Kansas City, Missouri where we stayed another 4-6 months in the hottest apartment I had ever been in. We had an inside small unit that had two windows opening up against a brick wall. Once again Bob spent most of his nights away from home on base duty so I worked as a R.N., I had now taken my state-board exams and had risen in ranks. I had no car so car-pooled with a male nurse and his wife back and forth to the hospital. They were the only friends I had, and yet it was strictly a working friendship. On one occasion I had no money so knowing payday was the next day, I knocked on the door to ask if I could borrow $5.00 until the following day. They obliged and handed me $5.00. I never saw them again for they vanished that night. The FBI questioned me about them the next day...as they were professional counterfeiters, and so I'm certain the $5.00 used to pay for the movie was hot off the press. Somehow my trusting nature had almost gotten me in trouble, but I escaped unscathed.

Mother and Dad did drive to Kansas City to see me, but the heat was too much for Dad and they had to leave after a very short time. Before they left they did buy me a table fan, which helped some.

From Kansas City we went to New Bern, North Carolina and it was here that I got to know the man I had married. We lived in a tiny upstairs apartment owned by a kind Lithuanian lady, Mrs. Francis, and once again I worked as a RN in a small Catholic Hospital, unaccredited, which fact was not known to me at the time. I soon found out that I was the only RN in the hospital with the exception of one nun, and all others were aids and orderlies and all were administering medication including narcotics. I was given the responsibility of counting and recording the narcotics and signing the narcotic sheet. When I went to the Mother Superior and told her what I had seen with everyone giving and taking narcotics themselves including one of the staff doctors I was told to mind my own business and just sign my name that the narcotics checked out. Fortunately I called the Director of the School Of Nursing in Madison, Wisconsin to ask what to do and was told to "run, not walk away from that job or lose my license," so I immediately quit my job. This was my first introduction to corruption and cover-up and it made a lasting impression. Today I no doubt would continue to attempt to correct the wrong doing, but then I was just scared, young and inexperienced.

During this traumatic time in my life, I found I was pregnant and the thought of having a baby was so utterly new and exciting to me. Unfortunately my joy was not shared, as Bob was furious. He told me he had never wanted children and that he had planned after his discharge from the service to play golf as a pro on the golf circuit and therefore children would interfere. He also wanted me to either have an abortion or give the child up for adoption. Sick at heart, confused, and shocked, I kept this to myself while the tiny life grew within me. I knew I could never give up my flesh and blood and would never even consider such options. The next months were difficult as he spent most of the time at the base, as he told me a PFC draws round-the-clock duty, and I believed him.

I had made no friends and had very little for the baby on the

65

way, but Mrs. Francis did give me a kitten, which I soon found was a great comfort. Mother and Dad shared in the exciting news and never knew the pain I suffered, although I'm not certain that Dad hadn't read between the lines. The Farrels were equally excited and seemed overjoyed...in fact, only the Father was bitter about the prospect of becoming a Father.

When I was 8 months pregnant I entered a TV contest to win a Boxer puppy. He was of Champion-lineage, and along with the puppy there was a year's supply of food and numerous puppy needs. The contest was sponsored by Dr. Pepper and Sweet Peach Snuff and was a "hillbilly" musical program. I wrote four pages on why I didn't like the program and won the dog on constructive criticism. My landlady, Mrs. Francis, was so excited that her tenant was to be on TV that she invited all of her neighbors in to watch me on TV, where I had to appear and receive the Championship Boxer Pup. Obviously the letter, which I had written, was never read on TV but only the reason for the judge's choices was given. The dog was named Farrel's Tarr Heal after the state of North Carolina, and he was called Tarr, but as soon as I returned to our apartment with Tarr we were evicted because no dogs were allowed in the apartment. With one month before delivery and a 4-month puppy, it was not easy to find accommodations in a small southern town so we ended up out in the country renting a garage apartment from the County Sheriff. He lived upstairs and we had a terrible apartment below, filthy, with no locks on the door or windows, across from a lumberyard and me with no transportation and a husband that was gone most of the time. I tried to fix it up the best I could as we only had two months before his discharge, but looking back it seemed more like 10 years.

The first terrifying encounter was meeting two very seedy book salesmen that appeared at our door selling encyclopedias. Bob went to the door and told them we weren't interested and that they would have to move their car as he was in a hurry to leave for the army base. After they left I panicked, for something alerted me as to the danger ahead. After Bob left I called the sheriff and told him of my fear and concern and of my situation. The police department agreed to send an unmarked car to sit in the lumberyard for one night only and watch the home. Around midnight the men returned and were accosted by the police. They were wanted rapists and had been pursed for sometime. It was a horrible ordeal for me and I never related it to Mother and Dad as with all the worrying and protection they had given me for so many years, they could never see their daughter in harms way and alone. It may have been because of their deep concern that I too recognized danger and survived. The police gave me a gun and suggested I keep it in my drawer after the incident, just in case I should ever need protection again. Thank goodness I never had to use it as the sight of it frightened me beyond belief.

Having children at an Army base is anything but a happy experience...at least that was the climate and atmosphere in 1954. The base hospital was a quanset hut and it was a "take a number" situation, so I'd take a bag lunch and plan to spend the day. I never knew which doctor I'd see, but it was all we could afford. Fortunately for me Bob was home when I went into labor, as we had to drive 10 miles to the base. Upon our arrival I was told to "cross your legs and don't breathe until 7:00 AM as the doctor on now is a butcher." I must have done just that as Susan Dawn was born at 7:08 AM after five hours of not only enduring pain, but also fear in this strange unattractive place. I really don't remember any doctor at all, only that the delivery room was full of Corp men running in and out of the Delivery room to board up windows as Hurricane Ida was about to strike. I'm sure a doctor did deliver, but I was so embarrassed, scared, and alone that I only tried to black out the entire ordeal, which to this day is still nothing but a faint reality to me. My roommate at the base hospital had a baby girl that she named Ida after the hurricane, and I remember thinking that was a strange reason for selecting a name. Shortly after delivery a bell clanged and all patients had to go to the hall and pick up her own breakfast tray and after breakfast and return the tray to the hall, then make her bed and stand for inspection next to the bed. I remember thinking that I was confused for a service personal and not a patient. Late morning the Corpman brought me Susan, a tiny 6lb baby, red and wrinkled. He was carrying her like a football under an arm and another baby under the other arm, no mask or gown, and I was appalled. The second day we were discharged and Susan was very sick as she was covered with Herpes in her mouth as well as the pelvic area. An epidemic was going thru the newborn nursery, so upon discharge I went right to a pediatrician's office, Dr. Graham Barden, who I credit with saving Susan's life. She was vomiting and so sick, and not only required IV's, but soybean milk. Her little mouth was painted purple with Gentian Violet as was her little bottom, and as I look back I know I would have handled such a terrible situation much differently today, and would have pursued investigations into such a filthy environment, but I was young, inexperienced and scared, and extremely grateful that Dr. Barden was my Savior and saved my adorable, precious little baby. Susan Dawn became everything to me...a dream of a baby and I couldn't have been happier for now I had someone to love and someone who needed me. Bob remained at the base, as he really wanted nothing to do with either of us. Mama Liz came down to see Susan, but left in a rage when she saw the way we were living in a garage, impoverished with nothing but a cat, dog and a baby.

The last incident before leaving our fateful abode happened during another hurricane. Once again Bob was gone and the Sheriff had given us keys to his upstairs apartment if ever an emergency arose. I was feeding Susan when I heard a rushing of water and looking up and saw the ceiling start to bulge while outside the winds and rain were fierce. I put Susan, Tarr, and Misty on our bed and put all the blankets, rugs and anything else I could find in front of the bedroom door and called the fire department. Since we were living in the country they were reluctant to come, but while on the phone, the ceiling collapsed and 250 gallons of hot water came rushing down. When the fire department arrived they found me hysterical, carrying furniture outside in the rain and running thru water with live electrical wires hanging from the ceiling. Bob was called home on an emergency and we were taken to the New Bern fire station. When the Sheriff was located he screamed at me for not starting a fire in his waste basket as he had fire insurance, but not flood damage so he lost everything downstairs. A rusted out water heater had broken loose. The next two weeks before Bob's discharge found us living in squalor in a musty smelling apartment where we stayed mostly on the screened porch with the baby and pets. Uncertain of the future I knew I must get back up north and close to Wisconsin if I was to survive.

Upon discharge Bob's Father had arranged for Bob to pick up his HFC job, only this time it was out of Freeport, Illinois and they had also leased an old farmhouse on the Haney estate for us to rent. The Haney's were two wealthy spinsters who owned a large hearse company as well as many parcels of land around Freeport. They took an immediate liking to me with my very small infant daughter and would send their car down to pick us up frequently for lunch or to swim in their pool. Our farmhouse was charming and I liked being in the country with farm animals. Mama Liz had decorated and furnished the interior home and I believe David Farrel was paying the rent, so all in all I felt life was wonderful. I even planted my first garden, which soon became over grown, and had to be dug up after I found snakes.

The year following our move to Freeport, I became pregnant which was more than Bob could tolerate, He had not wanted Susan, and now another. Again HFC meant working days and nights on end and often he was gone for a week at a time and I was left with no transportation, living in the country. My only friends were the Haney sisters, in there 80's, but yet I had Susan and I was happy. David Farrel drove to Freeport from Madison frequently and always came with groceries and gifts. Mother and Dad made it two or three times but never did I let on about my concern of Bob's where-about or his loathing of children and yet I do think Dad knew.

On March 21st, 1956 I delivered not one, but two adorable twin daughters. How different it was from my first delivery as now I was in a beautiful hospital and had a handsome private doctor, Dr. Lucas, who delivered the twins 8 minutes apart, Darcy Barnes weighed 6lb 14oz, and Debby Blair weighed 6lb 4oz. They were dark haired precious and healthy from the beginning and all four grandparents were ecstatic; however Bob was obviously disenchanted and still talked of putting all three up for adoption. I knew he was mentally ill and needed medical attention, but where to go for help. Our marriage was deteriorating at a rapid pace and he was never home, and never did I know his whereabouts until a letter came one day with a return address from Sterling, Il. I recognized what I thought to be a woman's handwriting so I decided to open the letter. The contents were very distressing; as he was being thanked for the beautiful jewelry and also was told she was counting the days until his return. Hurt and confused I managed to rent a car and drive to Sterling with the three babies in the car. The twins were three months old and Susan was twenty-one months old. I found the address and approached the door only to have a young woman with red curly hairs answer the door. She was probably in her 20's and when I introduced myself as Mrs. Robert Farrel, she insisted it must be another Bob Farrel as she had an engagement ring had been engaged for over a year and was looking forward to becoming his wife. It was then that I produced his picture and asked her if it was the same man. I must say I almost felt sorry for her as she burst into tears and we held each other in the doorway, one sobbing more than the other. We carried in the babies and had an eye opening conversation in which I found that he had been living with her for almost a year, but traveled in his job. When I later left to drive back to Freeport it was as though my world had crashed around me, and yet my three tiny daughters kept me from disaster. For a brief time I really contemplated ending my life, but then what of the children, my parents, and realized that I had to make plans for the future without Bob.

I called David Farrel who came down immediately as I was beside myself, sick for what I had married. He was womanizing monster, lying and cheating his whole life and robbing me of a Father for my small children. When Bob arrived home and was approached by his Father and myself and all the evidence, he looked straight at us and denied everything. It was at that moment I realized what was different about his eyes...they never really looked at you, but rather thru you and to some distance beyond, a strange look of someone lost.

Farrels decided that the only way to control Bob and help him was to move us back to Madison. They bought us a lovely Designer Showhouse on the west side of Madison in a quiet area. They completely furnished it and bought me my first car, a used car, but at least one of my own. Whether it was a bribe or a sincere gesture of love I'll never know, but I did love the Farrels. Bob was breaking their hearts and David especially was fearful of what I would do. He stopped by daily, but I knew I had to plan my life without Bob so I decided to go back to the University of Wisconsin to get my Ward Management and Teaching Degree. Farrels agreed to anything to keep me happy, so I hired someone and started back to school, setting a course for the future, that of a single Mother with three small children.

During this time Bob was drinking heavily, spending vast sums at the Maple Bluff Country Club and his Father kept bailing him out and footing the bills however, I no longer cared, as my course was charted, and so I studied, attended classes and was a quality Mother whenever possible. It was a struggle, but I knew what had to be done and so I kept a firm course, never letting on to anyone, I had a wonderful farm girl as a live in and Jeannie was very good to the babies and that is all I needed, so without love, and without any social life of any kind I pushed onward. Bob also pushed onward and finally thru despair and disappointment David Farrel suffered a fatal heart attack. This ended any hope for Bob, as Mama Liz couldn't face the reality of her son and was too ashamed to face what a scandal would do, but scandal or no scandal the time had come for now I had my degree and it was time to call my Father. I asked him to please come right away, and the urgency in my voice brought him down immediately and I told him the whole story, of my fear for our safety from this violent drunken womanizer who had brought nothing but shame and heart ache to all who loved him! Dad never reminded me of my terrible judgment, but only went on to lovingly protect his own. Locks were changed and an attorney immediately filed papers for a divorce, which offered Bob exactly what he wanted, freedom, complete with no child support and no support payment of any kind. This was in exchange for a signature that he would surrender any right to ever attempt to see his children or his ex wife again. He gladly signed, so much like an annulment, he walked away; the Father of three little girls and to his date has never attempted to contact any of us. A pathological liar, a lost soul, whatever his problem he was now out of our lives forever. Dad and I moved all of his belongings out of the home and told his attorney he had 48 hours to pick up his things or they would be donated. The possessions disappeared during the night and the handsome Prince Charming that had swept an impetuous emotional girl off her feet was gone, buried forever.

Dad remained for a few days while I tried to re group, Mother also came down and I found a wonderful RN position at Methodist Hospital in Madison. The Director of Nurses was a wonderful, caring human being, who took pity and a real liking for me. Ann Geyer became one of the dearest persons I would ever meet. She offered me two jobs, both salaried, evening supervisor from 3:00 to 11:00 PM, which offered more money, and an AM instructor in

Urology and Pharmacology, so I was now drawing two checks. Soon I was also made student advisor, which also was a paying position, and so with this I was able to make the mortgage payments and pay Jeannie, while Mother paid the utilities and milk bill. Dad offered all the love, advice and sympathy a loving Father can give and on one visit he handed me a check to cover all my college expenses for the year I went back to school. I was so shocked, but he said he wanted to know that I was sincere in my choice and had proven it, and therefore he wanted to feel he had given me my entire education. Coming from a poor, hard workingman, I was very grateful.

Time passed and my social life was nil except for Ann Geyer who weekly would arrive to treat me to an afternoon of golf, lunch, or a movie. She also managed to bring goodies for the children and even treats for the dog. I'll never forget the kindness of that dear sweet lady.

Occasionally, I would get a call form a married doctor or another visit from my first flame, Jim Nagle, but now I had a different outlook on life. I had grown up and what I needed was stability, a real home and love without condition.

On my own with three little girls

A Fresh Start

Ray and I on our wedding day

The date was September 7, 1958 and Mother and my dear Aunt Orliene had come to Madison to share in Susan's fourth birthday by taking the train to Chicago for her birthday present. We had never been on the train and Jeannie was at home with Debby and Darcy, so the four of us set off on a train adventure that was to change our lives. We were having lunch at the Walnut Room at Marshall Field when Mother suggested that I call that "nice Ray Busch". I told Mother that I hadn't seen him for years and no doubt he was married at which time she said, "No he's not, I've been writing to him for several years, ever since he left you at the University of Chicago and you returned the sweater. He wrote and told us what a fine moral girl you were and how fond he was of you, so we became pen pals and all the time he was in Korea in the service I sent care packages and wrote to him about you, your happy marriage, about Susan and the twins". I was shocked beyond belief, and as she continued on, I just sat dumb founded. She had never told him of any problems in the marriage or to my divorce but just quit writing. Mother always believed that if you didn't have anything nice to say then say nothing at all. She suggested that I call his parents in Skokie for his telephone number, gave me a dime, and said, "Now go call." I must say my heart skipped a beat when his Mother answered the phone, remembered me and told me he was a bachelor attorney living in Chicago with two other attorneys, gave me his number, but also said that I might not be able to reach him as he was on his way to Acapulco. I called, only to have him answer the phone. Seems the others had gone on ahead as he had forgotten something...he returned to the apartment to hear the phone ringing. Shocked, he said he would meet me under the Marshall Field's clock as he'd like to meet my Mother and see Susan, but would only have five minutes. The time was ever so short and sweet and so began a wonderful meaningful courtship that ended later in marriage. During that time Ray never missed a weekend to drive to Madison where we'd spend quality time with the children. They all adored him, especially Susan, who was asking every man if he'd be her Daddy. She now had found someone who said, "I hope so." Our relationship grew and soon the plain, quiet, stable man of few words and gentle ways became a giant in my eyes. He wasn't a flash in the pan. I had had that, but a truly caring person. Mother immediately liked Ray, but Dad held his judgment as his three little granddaughters had to have the best and my judgment had

Proud parents at wedding of Jenese and Ray

Wedding with children

been so poor the first time. Soon Dad too realized that Ray would be the stability needed for a good life and he gave his blessings on our marriage October 8, 1960.

It was a very small wedding; our three daughters, ages 4½ and 6 were my attendants as was Ruth Busch, my sister-in-law. Carl, Ray's only brother, was his best man, and those in attendance were the two sets of parents, my Aunt Orliene, Aunt Min and Aunt Louise and Carl's three children, Pam, Chris, and Skip. I remember discussing the dinner plans with Dad and offering to pay for half of the wedding dinner at the Orrington Hotel in Evanston, but he only smiled and told me he could afford to pay for such an important dinner. Out of respect for my Father we had no alcoholic beverages and only an ice water toast, which was appropriate... pure and clean, as was my life to be.

Unlike my first marriage, Ray and I discussed children and he said, only after he felt the girls were really and truly his did he want another child. Religion was another issue, but he thought it would be no major problem as he had always been a Baptist and I grew up in the Lutheran Church, so we decided to compromise. This is perhaps the only weakened area of our marriage as no compromise was ever agreed upon after the wedding. He told me that he could never leave the Baptist church as long as his Mother lived. She in now 97 years old and religion has been a sore subject and a definite weakness in the marriage and one that now offers challenges.

Our honeymoon was a storybook form beginning to end, saying goodbye to our three little girls...all staying with their new Grandmother, Frieda Busch, while we drove to New England and upstate New York. Fall is a beautiful time of yeas to visit New England and not only the scenery was awesome, but the antique shops were dotting the countryside. We stopped every few miles to add another new antique to our newly established home. By the time I added a spinning wheel, I realized the patience of this wonderful man. Our first unscheduled stop was at the home of Dr. Jarvis, a folk doctor living in Barre, Vermont. Ray had a very bad cold and the proprietor of an Inn that we stayed in recommended Apple Cider Vinegar and Honey, as suggested in the book written

A new Daddy... with love

by Dr. Jarvis. While driving t h the countryside we stopped by at an apple stand where not only were they selling apple cider, but also the best seller written by Dr. Jarvis. Reading the inner cover aloud to Ray, I discovered his homestead was in Barre, so when the marker on the road said Barre, only 25 miles off the beaten path, why not. We arrived at the home of Dr. Jarvis at 8:00 p.m. and were met by a lovely gracious Dr. and Mrs. Jarvis who invited us in for tea and conversation as well as an autograph of my newly purchased book. Dr. Jarvis told us that he had written his book as a legacy to his grandchildren, much as I am doing, and in it he shared all the folk medicine he had collected during his decades of being a country doctor.

From Vermont we ventured on to Martha's Vineyard and to the cape, all without reservations or plans, Driving on the Cape at night can prove hazardous especially if you haven't eaten and have a vivid imagination. I learned early on that my husband could suffice on two meals a day. The evening meal could be anytime between 7:00 and 10:00, but on the Cape everything closes early, so although our evening meal was supposed to be very special and romantic, ours was a real "one of a kind". The only establishment we found open was a streetcar converted to the "Maple Diner", dirty, empty and run by a kind, toothless lady, unskilled in the art of the culinary. I realized the only food that seemed free of ptomaine would be canned tomato soup, crackers, and a carton of milk. When the waitress, who was also the cook, showed concern about adding milk to tomato soup, Ray went behind the counter and made the soup while the waitress proceeded to empty a whole box of soda crackers on a large plate. No sooner had Ray sat back down when the door to the diner opened and in walked two men with guns strapped to their thighs. At this point I asked Ray to please open my carton of milk for me as I was trying to conceal my diamond ring with this armed "bandit" sitting next to me. Wondering about the gunman, I suggested in a whisper we leave immediately while the plate of crackers, bowl of soup and emptied carton remained on the counter. We paid and left quickly after which I informed Ray of our possible fate at the hands of two gunmen in an isolated place. My mind was racing with what ifs...and so we left.

Our motel on the Cape was at the top of an incline from the parking spaces and a light snow was falling so after waking the attendant and crawling under the covers, my vivid imagination took over and soon Ray was carrying spinning wheel and antiques up the hill in the snow so Jenese could get a good night's sleep. I kept envisioning those two men taking all of the treasures from our car. There are many ways to say "I love you", and his undying patience spoke to me constantly. Two more memorable encounters happened on our Honeymoon, both challenges at the time, but fun to recollect. First was our arrival in New York City without reservations at 1:00 A.M. No problem, was always Ray's attitude. He headed for a pay phone and after several call, we checked into the LaGuardia Airport Motel and were told that check out was 6:00 A.M. I had seen my husband in battle somewhat before, but never like this and he finally won his case and extended our check out to 9:00 A.M. however, the vacuuming started outside our room at 7:00 so between the take off and landings and the vacuuming, we did not have a restful night. The second challenge was likewise in New York City and again involved hotels. We had purchased a current book on hotels, their rates and locations and it showed that in downtown Manhattan there was a rate of $5.00, so I was to negotiate while Ray would circle the block. Driving around the block in New York City is no easy feat, but then renting a hotel room for $5.00 is even more impossible. The desk clerk looked at me as though I was crazy, but with my insistence, my booklet and the threat of Better Business Bureau, a hotel manager appeared, had words with the desk clerk and I was told there was only one room available at that price and did I care to see it. I politely said, "No, we'll take it," and proceeded to find Ray and tell him the good news. The entire staff watched with awe as Ray carried in our treasures, including the spinning wheel to our room. It was a room that I feel had quickly been converted from a broom closet as the room held only a bed, which filled the entire room. The bathroom was functional with a shower, commode and basin all tucked in. We managed rather nicely in a compact fashion as the antiques took over the shower stall when we didn't, and likewise the bed when we weren't in it. We managed two nights at these luxurious accommodations and I'm certain we were the "talk of the town" for years after we left. We've stayed in many places since that night, some of the finest hotels in the world, but our three nights spent in New York City on our honeymoon have to be the most memorable. Upon our return from our honeymoon we settled in Mount Prospect, Illinois in a new home, one of four models offered by a builder. The price was $40,000, near Skokie and also near the expressway leading to Chicago. We sold the Madison home for $28,000 under land-contract and started life anew as a new family on the block, complete with three children, a cat and a dog. Life with Ray and the three little girls now seemed like utopia after what I had gone thru with my first marriage...the many lonely hours of tears and frustrations...fearful of tomorrow, but having to press on for the children's sake. What made me go on from day to day was an inner strength I gathered and always remembered the words of my Father saying "we're tuffies and can always forge ahead." Soon after we took up residency in Mount Prospect we decided it was time to legally change the children's last names and Ray legally adopted the three little girls. We met in a judge's chambers in Chicago where the judge had three helium filled balloons and as they were released toward the ceiling the judge asked the children to raise their hands if they wanted to become Ray Busch's daughters, and so it was that our family was established. By the time Susan was eight years old we decided to increase our family and on June 1st, 1962 Nancy Rae was born, an adorable little baby, and as Susan stated, "I now have a twin sister." What proved to be almost feasible, as with the twins Susan was always on the outside looking in, and it seemed no matter how hard I tried, the twins only wanted each other. From the time they

A new addition to the Busch Household– Nancy Rae Busch

were delivered, the need for the other was apparent. The first night home from the hospital both Debby and Darcy cried endlessly and nothing seemed to console them until I got the brilliant notion to put the two together in one crib, and so it was one play-pen and one of whatever they touched. When six months old they were finally separated and put into separate cribs, but the cribs had to touch so they could feel each others' little hands thru the bars. Their closeness seemed to be to the exclusion of Susan even though she was only 1½ years older. Susan became "Mommy's little helper" and was constantly following me and did what I did, but her life did have that early rejection by her sisters, which has carried thru to this date, and she has never felt the closeness to Debby or Darcy as she feels for Nancy. As years passed Susan became her Father's idol and visa versa, as he too found a somewhat rejection from the twins, but I always claimed it was only characteristic of identical twins, but never did I really investigate the issue. We seemed a perfect, happy family always sharing all experiences, trips, holidays, school events, and life in general. Our life as a new little unit was full of love and happiness. The girls were our lives and never did we go or do anything without them. Ray so fit into the family as the Father, that our neighbors and newly made friends had no idea of our background, and so life was indeed happy. Mother and Aunt Orliene came down frequently on the train and all seemed comfortable with Ray, however, my Father on the other hand still reserved his ultimate judgment until Ray could prove himself, Dad never pointed out any flaws, but he could really only love his flesh and blood and since Ray was not flesh and blood, he could only earn my Father's respect. I believe Dad did see a rather weak man, led by a strict Mother and tied to the Baptist tradition...a man who would conform and not challenge adversities...a man of few words, without wit and charm, which was my Father, but also a man who adored his daughter and granddaughters and this must have given Dad great comfort as he watched carefully from afar. When Dad and I were together we always had our private walks, hand in hand and he would paraphrase in a philosophical way what his heart had to say. I longed for his approval and words of wisdom. His letters to me were frequent and always closed with, "love and hugs for Little Honey, the Darling Doubles, and Princess Shining Hair, and my regards to Ray." Mother and Dad drove down on occasion, Mother was still working at the factory and Dad putting in long hours as a sales representative for many small companies in his Package Display Company. Ray's position as Associate Legal Council for the University of Chicago had a very important ring to it, but compared to the salaries of private practicing attorneys, his salary was much less. He had attempted private practice when he first finished law school, but was unable to be successful. He needed to have a stable, salaried 9:00 to 5:00 job without too much stress or challenge and this he had at the University for 38 years, with a few financial bonuses, but far less than other attorneys. His one large bonus was free tuition for any of our children to any college or University in the United States for four years. This was

A Southern Colonial dream home

worth a great deal of money as it was tax free and offered all four of our daughters excellent education at the college of their choice. His salary covered our expenses, but left little for entertainment or trivial things so I decided to help out, not as a nurse because of the demanding hours, but rather in the fashion field, of which I had only the training obtained while at the University of Wisconsin at Bruce and Co. Innovation was always my forte, and with my Father's mastery reality, I had learned the art of shopping from my Father. How often I had gone shopping with him for a large purchase such as Mother's refrigerator, her Singer sewing machine, or her large white electric range. I always refer to the items as hers as this was the one present she would get every Xmas, and as I became a teenager I could tell Dad exactly what Mother wanted and I would always pick out the best for her and then watch Dad bargain. He would always pay cash, never charged anything nor did he believe in credit, so therefore carried a small bag of cash and explained to the salesclerk that is all he could pay, and would always succeed in purchasing the item at his designated figure. I had even seen Dad pay cash for his panel car that way, and he would say to me, "It's not what you earn, but what you save that counts," and so now as an adult with such a Master teacher, I set out to buy my dream car. I narrowed the field to either an Oldsmobile or a Buick, did my homework and withdrew the money from the bank, carried $100.00 bills in a small bag and left to see the Buick dealer in Mount Prospect, Bill Cook Agency. I carried $5,000.00 in cash and Ray refused to go with me as he said it was ridiculous and an impossible offer. But I knew I could do better on my own. I'll never forget the look on the salesman's face when I laid out my proposal. I wanted a "new 1973 Buick Centurion Convertible with a Cadillac color, "Metallic Gold", as I didn't like any of the Buick colors. I told the salesman that I also needed air conditioning, under-coating to protect from the winter salt on the streets, an AM-FM radio, deep gold carpet with four extra mats and all the money I had was $5,000.00 to include tax and license. I then laid out the $5,000.00 all in $100.00 bills on the desk and watched the salesman's reaction as he told me it was impossible to accept my offer. At this I politely thanked him for his time and started to pick up the money as the blood just pounded in my veins. How often I had seen Dad do the same thing, but then I was such a novice at this, when I suddenly heard the man say, "just a moment young lady, I'll be right back." I knew now I had a chance, but I must hold true to my course and while planning my next step a tall refined man entered the room and was introduced as the owner. He proceeded to stare at the money and at me and again I told him that I did not want to waste their time, but this is all I had or could get, so I'd gladly leave if it wasn't possible. I'll never forget the look on his face as he picked up the money and said, "Little lady, you just bought yourself a Buick Centurion Convertible." I wanted to leap up and hug him, but remained calm until I left the dealership and then I showed my exuberance. Ray couldn't believe it when I told him what happened, but from that day on I do all the buying of large items from cars to homes as I had learned so well from my Father. The wait for my beautiful convertible seemed endless but when it finally arrived I wanted to share it as well as my wonderful story with my Father, so Nancy and I drove to Eau Claire. Nancy was 13 years old at the time and so bubbly and full of enthusiasm and I remember reaching Eau Claire and driving to a filling station where we carefully washed away any dust or dirt from the 300 mile drive. Mother and Dad's reactions were totally different. Mother was so upset that I had bought a convertible as now she'd wow forever that I'd flip over and be killed. I explained to her that convertibles rarely flip over as they are much heavier cars and by today's standards, it's built like a tank. Dad loved it, especially with the white top down as he could feel the fresh breeze as we drove t h the countryside. Dad and I went for the ride and Nancy stayed behind with Mother to console her as she said she'd never ride in a convertible. As I told Dad of my bargaining and tremendous bargain he just beamed as he told me how very proud he was of me. We giggled together and he said he couldn't have done it any better and squeezed my hand, and I could see the pride in his eyes.

A great opportunity opened up in Mt. Prospect with the building of an 85 store mall. I immediately appeared in the corporate offices to see if they needed a Fashion Coordinator to represent all the stores in Mall Fashion Shops, presented a resume showing my experience at Bruce & Co. and after an interview with the Promotion Manager, Richard McCarthy, I was given the job. Two large shows were scheduled, Spring and Fall, and several specialty shows during the year such as "The Leather Industry Show," "Holiday Show," "Easter Parade" and on and on. I presented them ideas, furnished all models, narrated, and was in charge of the Fashion Department. Occasionally I would also do shows for the individual stores. My job as Fashion Coordinator, which lasted for 12 years, was exciting and fun and since I selected all the models, I chose to use our four daughters as the children's models and interviewed adults and teens for the job. Occasionally I would use professional models from the Models' Bureau when we had a celebrity guest or a specialty show that called for professional models.

One opportunity led to another and soon I was offered the position of directing a charm school for Montgomery Ward, one of the three department stores in the Mall. This I could do and still keep my Fashion Coordinator position so I now had two jobs, each equally exciting, and each involving my own daughters. As Director of the Wendy Ward Charm School I was sent on a Teen Fashion Tour to Europe for three weeks. The tour included such fashion capitals as London, Paris and Rome, and since my trip was an all-expense paid tour and I did get a discount on my own daughters I decided to take Susan, Debby and Darcy, all teens at the time, on the tour as well. My sister-in-law, Ruth and my two nieces, Pam and Chris also went, so the tour of 22 had seven Busch members on it. The entire tour was fabulous and the experience of sharing this with my own daughters added to the enjoyment. At the time I was working in fashion I became involved in Pageants as well, developing a local Pageant, training students for Pageants and introducing our own daughters to the Pageant world. It was during this busy time of my life that I was approached by a modeling agency in Chicago to register the twins who were now four years old, adorable with dark curly hair and soft brown eyes, and an innocence that shown thru their sparkling smiles. Susan was a beautiful little blonde with blue eyes who often went unnoticed because all attention was always given the twins. I remember on one occasion when we were dining out that some people stopped at our table to comment on what beautiful little twins, Susan stood up and said, "I'm Susan and I'm five years old." I realized how thoughtless and unthinking some people are not to acknowledge all the children in a group and leave out only one, but we always attempted to cover other people's blunders. The thought of permitting the children to model was appealing, but only if all three were a part of the modeling field.

The modeling field was completely different from the runway modeling I had known in Madison, as now it was both exciting and lucrative, especially if TV commercials were involved, but with rewards there are also expenses and Union dues, so soon after the first on camera work, the twins were required to join both AFTRA and SAG, two acting unions. Susan never did a commercial, but nonetheless every job was just as important as another and all the rewards were the same...another Barbie doll or accessory. The day arrived when an emergency arose and a Mother was needed on the set, and so I too plunged head first into on-camera work, not as frequently as my daughters, but still I was going to auditions and paying union dues. Like Susan, I gave each audition my all and on some occasions was chosen for the role. The one that will always remain uppermost in my mind was a Documentary film entitled "The Final Touch". It was a public service documentary to be shown to hospital therapy training classes as well as paramedics, showing the art of resuscitation and the use of the Heimlich. At the end of the audition I was told to play act by sitting at a table and cough until I choked and fell on the floor. For this acting part I had dressed up, fixed my hair and make-up to look my best at 9:00 AM, but with the willful intent to persevere I started to cough and cough and choke and as I did I nearly passed out and fell on the floor. I didn't have to relate to them that I do have an exaggerated gag reflex and so the choking came by naturally. Needless to say I was chosen for the lead part of Ruth and off I went to Milwaukee for three days of coughing, choking, and falling on the floor. It was a real trip in more ways than one, as I met the Director, Producer, and a cast of 35 extras, my stage husband, and two paramedics, one a bearded man with halitosis who had to deliver mouth to mouth resuscitation. The setting was an Italian restaurant rented exclusively for the filming. The extras were other patrons eating at the various tables, a bartender, and patrons eating at the bar. My role was to enjoy a wonderful dinner with my stage husband as it was our anniversary. The make-up artist applied my make-up and hair style to make me very glamorous for my big moment. As I was eating a traditional Italian dinner consisting of salad, spaghetti and garlic bread, I started to choke on the bread. Everyone stared at me choking, but no one was able to help. Finally I was to collapse and fall on the floor. The rehearsal lasted for over six hours with me coughing, choking and falling on the floor over and over while the Director would tell others where to be looking and how to act. At last the Director called for one more time when with all the strength I could muster, I said, "Look I'm an actress and I have but one choke left so it's now or never." A quiet hush fell over the room as the Director stated, "Ok, you've heard her, this is a take." I don't know where I got the energy or nerve, but I knew I had to deliver the choke of the year as it was now or never I started to choke and choke and choke, tears flowed down my face and the next thing I remember I grabbed the tablecloth and fell to the floor. All the pasta, wine, dishes and food flew on the floor and it not only was a take, but I won the Miami Gold Award for my choke scene. The second day was worse than the first as it was to be the death scene. I was made up to look the part, gentian violet was put inside my mouth and lips, a blue-Grey make-up was applied to my skin, oil was sprayed on my skin and hair and ice water was sprayed lightly over me to appear like perspiration beading up as I lay crumpled on the floor. My arm was gushing blood from the broken wine glass which cut my am as I fell, so to create the effect, there was a pump placed in my sleeve which oozed out a dark red substance. All in all I literally looked like death had taken over, but the paramedics arrived in time to use the mouth to mouth resuscitation with the bearded paramedic. Once again I had to stand my ground and stopped the shoot long enough for someone to purchase Scope to be used before we continued. I also had to defend my honor as I refused to have my breasts exposed as they applied a sternal rub, although my blouse was torn off, but nonetheless my nipples were never exposed or I threaten to walk off the set. This was embarrassing to me but enough was enough. The final maneuver was to insert an airway into my throat causing me to vomit. The Director loved the reality of the scene, as I did vomit, and asked for a repeat when I violently objected to the airway, so only the front portion of the airway was slipped between my lips and a mixture of Minestrone soup and egg whites was injected into my mouth with a syringe so it was oozing out of my mouth and covering my hair. The scene only took eight hours, but I really thought I had given my life to save others. On the way back to the hotel I decided to stop at a supermarket for some shampoo. Never have I had such a reception as everyone disappeared from the store, all the lines at the cash registers disappeared as I simply stepped up to the cash register and paid for the shampoo and left, leaving everyone speechless. Sick as I was I laughed all the way back to the hotel, and I only wish I could have gotten pictures of the shopper's faces. The third day was an ambulance scene where I was whisked off to the emergency room by ambulance. All in all, it was my first and last film and an experience I shall never forget. Of the $250.00 I made, I spent about $150.00 recovering and doctor's bills, and I now have great respect for the stunt people on camera as this is the part they perform. Another very memorable film job thru the agency was less severe and sheer enjoyment as I was a stand-in for Geraldine Fitzgerald in the film "Harry and Tonto" staring Art Carney and Geraldine Fitzgerald. I had been watching Art Carney in the "Honeymooners" for years, so the thought of being on the set with this great actor was very exciting. My wardrobe consisted of a battered chenille robe and old tennis shoes, and I stood under hot lights at the Altenheimer Old Peoples Home in Chicago for each scene until the lighting was properly placed and then the actors would exchange places, but for this experience I would have gladly paid. I received a day's pay and a most wonderful opportunity to sit with Art Carney and Geraldine Fitzgerald at lunch. Art Carney was the most genuine human being. I asked him what he enjoyed doing when not performing and he said he liked to play the piano. Since there was an old piano on the stage, I asked him if he could please play something for us. The next hour and a half was enchanting as Art Carney, with his eyes closed, played one beautiful arrangement followed by another, and all connected with arpeggios. It was a beautiful private concert. The only ones upset were the producer and the director, Zero Mostels's son, who asked what dummy had ever asked Art Carney to play the piano as it held up the entire shoot, as no one dared interrupt the star. I loved hearing him and obviously never confessed to being the one that caused the long delay. I did have a few somewhat glamorous roles,

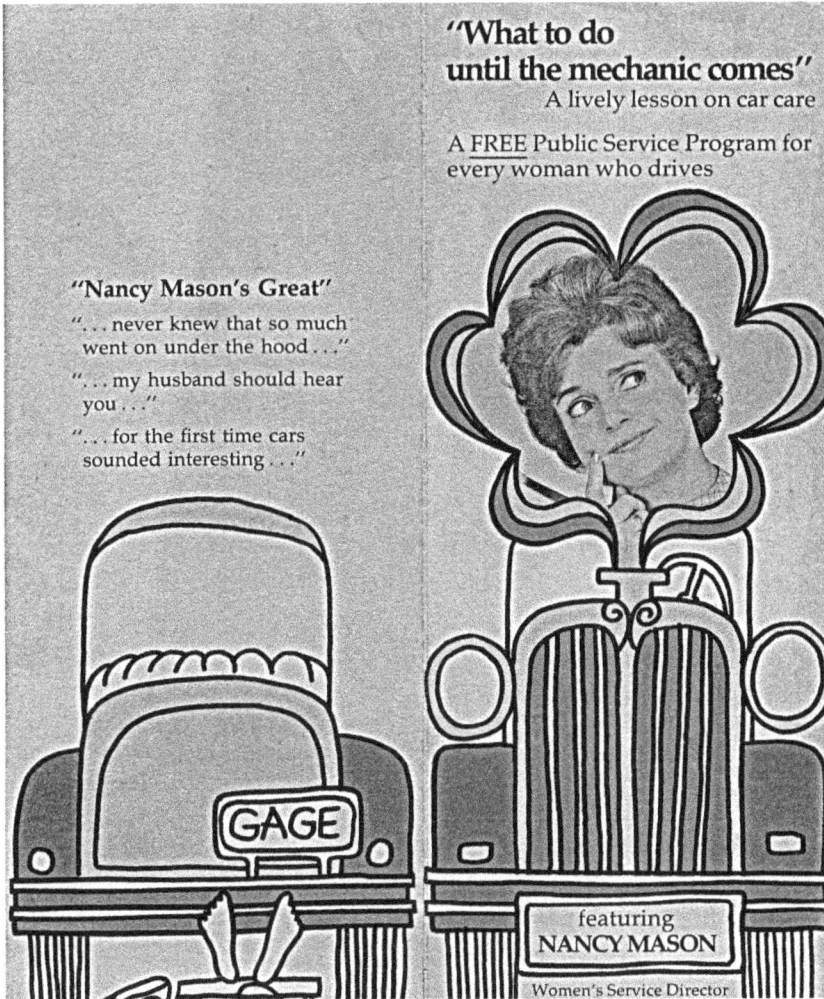

Not all modeling is glamorous.
Nancy Mason, the "lady" mechanic

one an Aunt in a Hallmark greeting card commercial, and another for Winston cigarettes, but unfortunately after the commercial was filmed, TV commercials on smoking were no longer shown, and so my commercial career was short lived. One job was way out of my league as I soon found out, but I handled it quite well considering. It involved the Chicago Syndicate, but at the time I had no knowledge of such. I was to meet the owners of a sporting goods Co. at the Sheraton O'Hare to discuss a convention to be held the next day. Representatives of the company were flying in for the meeting and my role was to present a narrated fashion show using six young female models supplied by an agency. Since fashion shows were my forte, this was no challenge, and I was told that I could request any salary as the owners were in a bind. I was not ready for the arrogant attitude and rudeness of the two men that interviewed me, but I acted as though I could handle any situation, so when they asked me what fee I wanted to do the show I immediately said $500.00. To me this was really big money and not what I was used to getting, and with this the men burst out laughing hysterically and told me that I could have asked for $5,000.00 and gotten it. One of them then offered me a job on "Tony the Tuna's Yacht" doing bikini shows. I refused realizing I was now talking to a mobster as I had read about Tony the Tuna. The next morning I arrived early at the convention center to meet the models. 17 and 18 year olds. After telling them what to wear and where to walk, we waited for the show to begin. The models had to change behind a large portable screen set up at one end of the banquet room and as I was narrating I kept seeing flashes go off, so I called for a 15 minute intermission and went back to see what was happening. A photographer was busy photographing the minor girls changing, mostly topless. With the now very angry older man demanding I go back and resume the show immediately, I held my ground and said I wanted my $500.00 cash immediately and the film and then and only then would I continue. Where I got the courage I'll never know, but I received the money and film, finished the show and left in a hurry, but I did look over my shoulder for months, and it made me leery of what job offers I should accept. Of all my modeling jobs, the one I enjoyed the most was the role of "Nancy Mason", a woman mechanic. I was sent on the audition because of my narrating ability, as I literally knew nothing about a car. This was to be a public service program sponsored by Chrysler, and I went into training at Mel Wolf's Car Agency. Presentations were set up for me by an Advertising Agency and I was to receive $35.00 per show, which doesn't sound very lucrative, but some days I was able to do two or three presentations a day. I had a script, a monkey coat and a brochure with me, "Nancy Mason", pictured on the front, as the "Lady Mechanic who would know what to do until the mechanic comes." I was able to change the script and put it into my own words as long as I covered all points, used flip charts and closed the program with a question and answer portion which soon was a real training tool for me, as often another member of the audience would answer the question, or I would take the name and number of the person asking the question, get the correct answer and return the call. In a very short time I found I really did start to understand some of the working parts under the hood. I learned to change and rotate tires and did live TV in front of an audience. I also was taught how to unstick a Butterfly valve and showed this on TV. Before the year was over I had presented over 100 programs in Illinois and Indiana. I really think it was the spirit of giving my all and acting with confidence that made the program successful. The same spirit I saw in my own daughters. Susan had always wanted to be a cheerleader but had never made the squad. One day the agency called and asked if Susan had been a cheerleader as they needed a cheerleader for an ad. Of course I did the honorable thing and said, "Oh yes, a great cheerleader." The next day she was booked for a shoot on-camera at a stadium where all she had to do was her jumps and cheer with enthusiasm. On-camera is all acting and I knew Susan had the will, which is the main part of acting. She was so excited and after borrowing a cheerleading costume we headed for the stadium. I'll never forget my beautiful Susan doing jump after jump, radiating with enthusiasm. The small audience watching exclaimed that they could see why she was a top cheerleader, which made Susan and I giggle all the way home. She had proven to be a real trooper or "Tuffie" as Dad would say. Each of the girls had the same kindred spirit as I recall a Hotpoint commercial. Debby had been chosen for the job, but had a problem with her right arm as she was undergoing therapy for her elbow which she had broken earlier that year in a bad fall. She was only nine years old at the time of the commercial, but no one in the advertising agency nor any of the camera crew ever knew that she couldn't completely straighten her arm as she loaded and unloaded the dishwasher with no indication of any problem. She loved role-playing and this was another play-day for her and she handled the job like a real pro. In time her arm did completely straighten, but not without a lot of determination and willpower from a young girl, and the willpower of two loving parents who worked the elbow routinely with exercise.

Darcy showed her true colors over and over, but the bride scene stands out the most as poor little Darcy would always get car sick when we drove anywhere, and so it was as we were on the way to Chicago where she was to model for the Marshall Field's Flyer...the Halloween bridal costume. She had been the bride the previous year as well as for the previous two years and each time the 22 mile trip upset her tummy. We'd stop, get a nice cool glass of water, put a little blush on her cheeks and be ready to wear the little white satin gown and veil...and enjoying every moment she was on camera. Nancy became our most successful model as she began at the age of 4 months with Commonwealth Edison commercials and was chosen without any audition. The Ad agency was at our home filming a Miles Lab shoot for "One A Day Vitamin" with Darcy when they spotted Nancy in her baby jumper chair, and immediately asked if she could do a commercial the next week, and thus her career began. She modeled for covers of magazines such as Parents, and also covers of catalogs such as Sear Xmas Catalog and J.C. Penny. Her outgoing personality and ability to take directions as a toddler and play act was past of the reason she won almost every audition she went to and she was also adorable with long silky blonde hair to her waist and a winning smile. The most outstanding job I remember for Nancy was her "Nine Lives Cat Food" commercial. She was three years old, was dressed in Dr. Denton pajamas rubbed from head to toe with catnip, which made the nine kitties in the commercial go crazy over Nancy, rubbing against her and purring. One of the reasons she was chosen over everyone else who auditioned was because we had cats at home and she wasn't afraid of animals, so in the audition when the auditioners let several cats out of cages, to observe the children's' reactions, most children ran out screaming, while Nancy remained in the room chasing the kitties. Her past in the commercial was to enter t h an open door and walk across the kitchen carrying a bowl of Nine-Lives-cat food. She was then to place the bowl on the counter without uttering a word, all the time, the cats were going crazy, and the announcer would do a voice over on film. After several rehearsals, they decided to attempt a shoot and Nancy came thru the door as directed, but walked to the middle of the kitchen, looked around and placed the bowl of cat food on the floor and looking into the camera she said, "But the kitties are still hungry". It was great...all watching the filming including executives from Nine-Lives, the Ad Agency, director, camera-men etc, were very excited and attempted to have her do it again, but only once would she perform this style. This is the one that was chosen to become a national commercial; however, no-one except myself and those at the shoot that day knew the commercial was rewritten by a three year old. The modeling jobs were many and each a new adventure with rewards. It was great training for the girls and not only taught them to follow directions, to have patience, to listen, and to act the part they were given. Each performed her role to the fullest and the later each seemed to excel in school or profession and I often attribute it to the fact that they had the wonderful experience of modeling, not as fashion models on a runway, although they did that too, but the on-camera work they did for magazines and commercials. The Agency seemed to type cast them in the proper roles as the twins were chosen, Darcy for her dreamy, far away look, her tenderness and love which radiated from her face. Debby was chosen for her spirit, a happy bubbly little girl that always seemed so light hearted. Even the "One-A-Day" people used the twins for two varying roles. Darcy was used for the ad at home with the little girl holding her rag doll and looking out the window waiting for her Daddy to come home. The dreamy look in her eyes was captured on film...how often over the years I have seen that beautiful look, so sad and yet so forgiving. Debby did the under-water action job for "One-A-Day Vitamin". Her role required all the spirit and courage a seven year old could muster. She was dressed in a party dress, Mary-Jane shoes with ruffled anklets, and wore her long dark curl flowing freely to the waist. All this was the setting while she was lowered into six feet of water in the swimming pool at the St. Charles Resort in St. Charles, Illinois. A lead weight had been put under her dress and sewn into the hem of her dress to keep it down while under-water camera crews filmed. Debby was holding a glass in one hand and a small red "One-A-Day" vitamin in the other, and the caption was to read, the vitamin that holds up under water. The entire pool was rented by Miles Laboratory and had been de-chlorinated so Debby could keep her eyes open under water. After hours of filming the job ended, only to be repeated the next day because the shots were too unbelievable, so the second day air machines were brought in and bubbles released around Debby as she stood on the bottom of the pool, eyes wide and open and smiling a large smile. She really was a wonderful little actress and loved the job...in fact when it ended she asked to stay in the pool and play. During their growing years I was chauffeuring the girls everywhere, but always enjoying each opportunity to be with them, and always encouraging them in their role-playing. Piano lessons began at the age of five for Susan and two years later for Debby and Darcy. Sue loved the piano and it became her special time to play and perform. With work and diligent practice she soon found music as a place to show her talent. Whatever the motivation, Sue went on to become an outstanding pianist, one of the best Mrs. Grady, her piano teacher, had ever had, She constantly won state awards and always made the Critics Circle in Guild Audition in which she performed yearly. Debby and Darcy liked piano but never took it as serious as Sue and at one point Darcy had even asked if she might quit the piano, but we encouraged her to continue thru High School. Nancy also started at the age of five and it is now rewarding to see each of our daughters playing the piano for their own enjoyment or encouraging their children to take lessons. School years were all met with good grades, very little effort, with the exception of Susan who had to work for her grades and took school more seriously than her sisters. Nancy was able to breeze thru anything and pull A's and superiors in everything and was able to excel with very little effort. During their high school years I became involved in the Pageant World, first thru the Wendy Ward Program where I taught students how to prepare for Pageants. I then chaperoned girls to national pageants, and finally started judging pageants both on the local and state levels. Susan was the first to enter a pageant and won "Miss Mount Prospect" and became 2nd runner-up in the "Miss Illinois" and 1st runner-up in the "Miss Indiana Pageant". Each time she performed Beethoven's "Pathetique" on the piano and won the talent award in each pageant. Although her talent was superior she never made it to the nationals, nor did Debby and Darcy although they also placed in the top five in the state level of the Miss Universe Pageant. Nancy was raised in a Pageant family, going to watch her sisters in many performances and she was always interested in seeing pretty girls compete, but she was young, overweight, wore glasses, had braces on her teeth, and was not quite pageant material, however, she did learn all the steps toward that goal, and when she was 13 she announced that she wanted to try out for the Miss Illinois Teenage Pageant. Knowing she didn't have a chance I did think the experience would be very good for her and it proved to be not only exciting for her, but I saw a very awkward girl with tremendous stage presence having a ball. She didn't place out of the 160 contestants, but opted to try again the following year if only we would give her contact lens. A growing step, it paid off as she now started to shed the pounds, take care of her skin and hair and became 4th runner-up in the state. She now announced that she would wait two years and try again. When a girl has such determination and such a plan with a goal, there is hope, and it was thrilling to see our beautiful Nancy crowned "Miss Illinois Teenager" and the opportunity to go to national and appear in the Teenage America Pageant. We all went to see her announced in the top five nationwide and see this beautiful young lady succeed thru sheer determination and hard work. I knew she was going to win as she was confident as well as radiant, and intelligent as well as vocal, so with such a combination I knew she would be difficult to defeat. College was next and we had three daughters at one time in college, all choosing DePauw in Greencastle, Indiana, a small Midwestern college with a great music school, as well as a great academic program for undergraduates. All three graduated the same day, Sue from Grad school and Debby and Darcy from undergrad, and the weddings started one week after graduation. Romances had been on and off again thru college, but Darcy's romance worried us, as she had fallen for the captain of the football team, a non-ambitious fellow on a full scholarship that seldom attended classes, and had no ambition for the future. After meeting him and realizing his saddened state we attempted to convince our daughter of her poor judgment. We also found out that he was on drugs and his background was far removed from the way we had raised our daughters. He had two sisters, both of whom had dropped out of high school to have babies. The more I attempted to discourage, the worse the matter grew until finally we decided I should take Darcy to Baltimore, Maryland to his home in Dundolk, the shipyard area of Baltimore, to meet his family. I drove the other three girls along and after meeting his family we left Darcy there for three days with his family while we went to the beach hoping she would change her mind. My plans almost backfired when I went to pick her up. Her boyfriend, Sam, had told her that she was to stay with them, and his Father came to the door, tattooed and drinking beer, and informed me that "what Sammy wants, Sammy gets, and he wants Darcy". How I managed to get Darcy out of there and in the car I'll never know, but soon we were doing everything to show her the finer things of life and what she would be missing. I had Ray immediately book a Cruise, bought the girls new clothes and soon the message got thru, and Darcy broke off relations with Sam. From here it goes from the frying pan into the fire with Darcy as she met a handsome, polished, wealthy fellow, president of the Student Body, an SAE and the 'Man on campus'. Rob Lukemeyer was a young Ryan 0'Neal and somehow I lost my Father's wisdom and saw only the surface, my Mother's passion for appearances and position. His Father owned a small chain of clothing stores, Roderick St. John, in the Indianapolis and LaFayette area. They had a beautiful country home complete with tennis courts and swimming pool and all I thought, anyone could ask for. Little did I know the back-ground of the Lukemeyers', but only saw the superficial aspects and a wonderful future for Darcy with a good provider who appreciated the finer things of life. Had I known that their social behavior of serving drinks and having cocktails at all times was the symptoms of alcoholics I might have advised Darcy differently. Two of his grandparents had died alcoholics, and his sisters were both alcoholics as was Rob. I remember staying overnight at the Lukemeyers and having Rob's Mother, Pat, prepare breakfast for us with a Martini in one hand. This was the weekend we stayed at the Lukemeyers prior to the wedding, a wedding that was picture perfect. To Darcy, marriage was forever...a fairytale romance ending in white silk and satin with flowers, champagne, and her 'White Knight' promising to love, honor and protect her always. He was not only an alcoholic, but an extremely sick individual who enjoyed pornography, which he himself filmed as a hobby as he performed sexual acts while taking pictures of himself. Darcy lived with this monster for the sake of the two children for 16 years during which time she suffered not only two ruptured discs, but also a brain aneurysm. At no time were we notified of Darcy's grave condition, but only called by Debby when she found out about it. The ruptured discs came early in her marriage, soon after the birth of Robbie, at that time Heather her daughter was two. Rob had his uncle who was chief-of-staff at an Indianapolis hospital make all the arrangements for a Chemopathic type of surgery which was approved in Canada, but not yet in America. The procedure failed, and another type of surgery was tried, this time in Dallas where thru the abdomen the two ruptured discs were removed and cadaver bones replaced.

Possibly they would have healed, but while in the hospital and in a body cast, Rob continually forced sex on Darcy, and the surgery failed. All of these truths were told me years later and my reaction was one of shock and despair, and if he had not already left her I don't know what I would have suggested. The final act of compassion came when she suffered a brain aneurysm and was in intensive care for weeks and yet we were not notified. I later found out that Rob had beaten her head against the wall when in an alcoholic rage. He did this more than once and I have always believed that he caused her aneurysm. Debby who was sent for finally called us and during Darcy's hospital stay Rob never once went to see her. Two years later he filed for a divorce. The secrecy, the pain and hurt has now come alive and we are all trying to pick up life's pieces caused by a vindictive, sick, abusive, raging alcoholic and although the divorce is over we are attempting to assist our daughter who was left penniless, without any support, nor any health benefits, as the Lukemeyer's closed their stores and claimed Chapter 11 as did Rob claim personal bankruptcy. When their plans were all laid, Rob filed for divorce. Everything was rigged from the attorney hired by Darcy to represent her to the judge who heard the divorce decree in Boone County, Indiana. He was a personal friend of Luke Lukemeyer, Rob's Father, played golf regularly with him as did the attorneys on both sides. In fact Darcy's attorney excused herself one week before the case was to be heard due to "conflict of interest" and left for Mexico. Our daughter was in the hospital when the divorce procedure was held without representation and after coaching by the Lukemeyers during the wee hours the night before the hearing, the children responded as they were told and the judge awarded custody of the two children to a raging alcoholic who in my mind with the photos I have in my possession, is also a sexual deviate. The sham is something one only reads about but this is factual and documentation will substantiate all that is written. The grades of the children suffered greatly when the children went to live with their Father in his new "bachelor pad" as he called it, with all new leather furniture etc. Darcy did receive the home which had a very large mortgage on it, no health nor hospital insurance, so without any funds she had to go on welfare and obtain food stamps and Medicaid, and we have been supporting her for the eight years she has been divorced. Heather's life has been turned upside down due to the influence of her alcoholic Father, his permissiveness in enabling her to drink, try drugs and stay out all hours, which has turned a beautiful girl with high morals into a free spirited hippie who has stolen from her Mother to buy drugs, has called her as well as me a "Bitch", and has caused Darcy so much mental anguish and pain that I believe there should be a penalty for the Judge as well as for the Father. Heather is now living with her boyfriend, is a young adult and I hope and pray will turn herself around as now she is lost...has quit college three times and is bitter with a questionable future, and is a confused young woman. Robbie is now in college and has been Darcy's strength as he has been loyal and true to her no matter where he had to live. He would sneak over to be with his Mother, and has often driven home from school in his old car, parked it far from Darcy's home and run home to spend the weekend with her. He hates his Father who has denied him everything, except tuition, which he has to pay for four years as ordered by the court. Heather likewise hates her Father and left with her boyfriend without telling him where she was going. He has lost both of his children, and the Lukemeyer's have lost their only grandchildren, but neither seem to be too concerned. Material possessions and parties still take over most of their lives or so I am told. Rob has remarried a woman with two children, and if his wife only knew...I try not to think of him at all, but I do hope and pray that someday Heather can show her Mother the love and respect she so deserves and I again can put her back in my Will, but as I write this book, I have completely disowned her and do so with a very heavy heart. Darcy's twin sister, Debby was also in love in college, but with only one throughout her entire four years at DePauw. When I first met Gary Cooper he was jumping on a trampoline in a Marathon for Sigma Chi. He was a rather big, heavy set fellow with a great smile, a strong face and a winning personality. He seemed to adore Debby and although he was one year older, he encouraged her to date others to be certain that she really wanted only him. Their wedding like that of her twin sister had eight bridesmaids and a barrage of guests as all the Sigma Chi's attended and sang the "Sweetheart of Sigma Chi" to Debby as she radiated in her beautiful gown. Her life wasn't a road paved with riches like that of Darcy, but a road paved with love and it is still moving on. She has suffered many traumas in her marriage, but Gary remains there for her. The first trauma was seeing Darcy in such a mental state after her back failures, her aneurysm, and finally a nervous breakdown. With all the pain of an identical twin, Debby also suffered the pain and although it wasn't physical, it was real and emotional and she too suffered a nervous break-down. Darcy's break-down was caused by life with a raging alcoholic, but the psychiatrist who cared for Darcy instead worked on a "FMS" Syndrome, of which I had never heard. Debby's psychiatrist also found that the "Forgotten Memory Syndrome" was the cause for any suffering in later life, so now our entire life as a family became one of child abuse, neglect, unhappiness and all because their original Father had been taken from them. I had no idea of what was happening and why Debby and Darcy were turning away from us, but I started wondering when we were never notified about Darcy's serious illnesses, only later to find out that Rob had told the psychiatrist and Darcy that she not be allowed to see or talk to us, and she was so weak and despondent that she turned to Debby who suffered the same breakdown. Since the nightmare that affected our entire family I have found that this is common among many psychiatrists to work on the minds of emotionally unstable persons, and somehow twist the truth and put notions and ideas into their minds that really become reality to them. According to the Psychiatrists, the fact that I had been divorced and Debby and Darcy had been denied the right to see their genetic Father had altered their lives and accounted for their emotional break-down. This has been extremely difficult for my husband, their real Father who adopted them at such a young age to comprehend, and the hurt and pain it has inflicted on our family has been unreal, but then as my Father always reminded me, we are "Tuffies" and can face anything, and so I have been strong thru all of the grief and frustration.

Darcy has come back into the fold and we are in constant touch with Darcy and are her sole support and she claims, "her best friends," the bond between Debby and the rest of the family is still strained. Gary has remained steadfast throughout and has been with her every step of the way. They have one little boy, Greggory, who is now eight years old and who I have only held a few times when he was a baby. He doesn't really know any of us, but is very close to his Father, who has to both Mother and Father to him as Debby has been almost bedridden for three years since a Mastectomy and breast reconstruction surgery done three years ago. Neromas have grown under the reconstructed breast and the doctors appear to be baffled as to how to best handle the constant pain suffered by Debby. Thru it all Debby continues to blame me for much of her suffering and pain all because of the "FMS" Syndrome and the denial of not knowing her genetic Father. I have suggested that she try to find him if it would help her, but I have had no contact with him since the twins were six months old and that was 40 years ago. I don't even know if he is still alive, but I know that his whereabouts could be traced. I listen to Debby and only hope and pray that she can regain her life before her little boy is grown and gone because she is missing out on so much of his life...but again, thank God for Gary.

Sue's love started with her appearance as "Miss Indianapolis" in the Miss Indiana Pageant. One of her duties as winner was to present the tennis trophy to Jimmy Connors. Michael Marsico, a long time friend of Jimmy Connors and an excellent tennis player who at one time taught tennis at Elmhurst College, was at the tournament as well. Susan called us from Indianapolis and told us that Jimmy Connors had offered to fly her back to Chicago in his private plane and Mike was also aboard. Mike was a handsome man of Greek heritage, somewhat older than Sue. He had been married before and claimed he fell in love with Sue on first sight. I had never heard Susan talk of marriage before and now she was talking seriously about falling for Mike. Much preparation had to be made in such a union, as Mike was Orthodox Greek and Sue was Methodist. Soon our beautiful blond, blue-eyed Susan was taking instruction and also learning how to prepare Greek dishes. Never did Sue enter into anything that she didn't put her heart and soul into what she was doing. Wedding plans were made for November and since we already had given one wedding for 330 persons for Darcy and had another one coming up in May for another 300 people, we were concerned about the monetary expense; however, how could we say no to Sue when we had blessed the other two announcements, so we told her that she could spend the same as her two sisters and somehow we'd survive three weddings in one year. Sue and Mike opted to have a very small wedding, immediate families only and use the money instead for a down-payment on a Condo. This was in agreement with us, but we hadn't foreseen a real problem and that was Mike's Mother. She was first generation Greek as her parents had come from Greece and everything had to be done according to Greek tradition. Everything was going from bad to worse and she insisted that all first cousins had to attend and so as a final peace offering, Ray and I decided to leave for the Orient for a short trip and leave his Mother, Exon Theape, better known in American terms as Ann, in charge along with Susan. At first Susan was devastated but we told her what she had to spend, and that unless his Mother had her way, Sue's chances for happiness with Mike were limited. I do believe that his Mother was responsible for breaking up Mike's first marriage of less than one year because she didn't like the wife. In fact she went so far as to give Sue wedding gifts from Mike's first marriage, unopened and addressed to the former bride. Ann had kept the gifts as they arrived addressed to Mike and his perspective fiancée in her closet because of her dislike for the fiancée. This included a complete set of ivory and gold china which to date Sue doesn't feel right using as it wasn't meant for her, but nevertheless it still is their fine china used for special occasions. A more difficult woman than Mike's Mother, in my estimate, is hard to find. We did go on our trip and returned four days before the wedding, which we paid for, but felt like guests as it, was all so foreign. There were 125 Greek people and 12 of us; however, it was a beautiful wedding ceremony where both Ann and I had an active part. We stood at the foot of the altar and tossed rose petals while Sue and Mike with joined crowns on their heads, followed by the Gumpa or Godfather, who is the best-man, circled the altar three times. After the ceremony, the reception was held at one of the Greek reception halls in the Chicago area and while Antonia and his magic violins, who were instructed by Ann to play only Greek music, played "Never on Sunday" over and over, guests engaged in handkerchief dances. It was one of the liveliest receptions I had ever attended. Before the wedding Ann had called all the guests and asked them; to bring a sweet for the "sweets table", one from their national heritage. When Ann called my Mother and asked her what her nationality was Mother said, "American," followed by, "No, you can't be just an American, you must have your roots elsewhere and that is the area that your sweet must come from." My Mother informed Ann that her ancestry stemmed from Scotland, but not knowing anything about Scottish cooking, Mother made brownies with pecans...which I thought was great. Everyone had a wonderful time and Sue and Mike got enough money from the Greek guests who flew in from Greece and presented them with cash placed in a large satin pouch which Sue had to hold open in the reception line. The cash covered enough to assist them with their down-payment of their Condo and his Mother was kept happy for a short time. The only problem is that his Mother has never stopped being in charge and has been a real thorn in their marriage since the beginning. It has caused Mike to break with the Greek church and a real feeling between Mike's Mother, Sue and the three children, Missy, Matt, and Mandy. It mostly started when the oldest was born and Ann insisted she name the baby. Mike told her that they were Americans first and Greek second and that he and Sue were going to name the baby. Melissa Dawn Marsico was born June 13th and although she was baptized in the Greek church, Ann did not attend, nor would she see or have anything to do with the baby. It took months before she even visited to see her only grandchild.

Nancy's marriage was preceded by a history of a very bright girl with an adventurous spirit; stubborn to a fault, and a love and passion for learning without compromise.

Although there were many platonic dates, there were only two real loves in her life. The first was a Spanish matador, Vicente Campos. She had met him while attending Columbia University in Seville, Spain during a DePauw exchange program. Although they appeared to be madly in love, the romance was doomed from the start as he spoke very little English and was the son of a wealthy rancher who raised bulls for fighting and who greatly resented any foreign females dating his son. He had already disowned one son for marrying a foreign girl, and he was not going to loose Vicente to an American. I had the opportunity to meet Vicente when I went to Europe at the end of Nancy's studies in Seville and could understand why she would fall for such a handsome, debonair young man who not only presented Nancy with a dozen roses upon our meeting, but also brought a dozen roses for "Mama", however I realized that their love was in vain. They continued to correspond across the miles upon her return to Chicago, and he phoned frequently, but soon she too realized that it was not to be and so a rather broken-hearted young lady now graduated and took her place in the professional world by entering the law school at Loyola. At first she was only half interested, as her heartache was still apparent, but soon she was engrossed in her studies and juries and graduated in the top 10% of her class of 148 at Loyola. During her time in law school she worked as an Intern at a large law firm in Chicago, Jenner and Block which had on staff of 250 attorneys. Her interest in law was now full-time as she met her second love, and pursued it until it resolved itself in one of the most beautiful weddings I have ever attended. Franco was tall, dark and handsome, of Italian descent, and our tall beautiful blonde daughter completed the stunning twosome. Their courtship was stormy, on again, off again for several years, but she never deviated from her course and at her wedding when she addressed the 300 guests, she mentioned that she had known for seven years, that which Franco had just found out, that they were meant to be together. The wedding was a "forever after" setting amidst beautiful European gardens, fountains, serpentine pools, and peacocks. Held at Montifiori Gardens, it encompassed acres of beautiful manicured gardens, white tents, lawn chairs with white satin streams, large cisterns filled with flowers while ivy and Hydrangeas covered a very large arch where the altar stood. Both a minister and a priest performed. Strolling violins played before the ceremony, at the service, and during the dinner. A 10 piece orchestra took over for the dancing after dinner. All in all it was a perfect affair to all that attended; however, no one really knew the tension and fear that set the backdrop for the wedding. Dear sweet Nancy; had dreams and visions of righting all the hurts and wrongs that were going on in our family since the FMS Syndrome had reared its ugly head. She believed that if her three sisters, her nieces and nephews were all in the wedding party, all hostile feelings would disappear. She was informed that Gregory, age four, Debby's son would not be in the wedding nor could he even sit with any of the family members nor could the husbands of the twins sit with the family, so with all these ultimatums the wedding was planned to be a most happy and blessed event.

On the day of the wedding, six bridesmaids arrived at our home for the traditional luncheon the day of the wedding, but the twins, and Heather, daughter of Darcy, were not there. Nancy had a brave smile as she welcomed her lifelong friends, her sister Susan and Sue's daughter, Missy. No real pictures can be taken with three of the bridesmaids missing, but the others posed in front of the home with Nancy and she maintained a smile, being ever so brave, not showing the anxiety and concern, and the uncertainty of the day, as a secret such as our is meant to be kept close within the family.

Stepping from the white stretch limousine, I felt my heart pounding as it was the first time in four years I had seen my twin daughters and my granddaughter. They were dressed in their beautiful ivory silk gowns and as the limousine drove up I stopped and said a silent prayer and stepped out slowly, wanting to rush and take them in my arms, but afraid to move. I really experienced my first feeling of stage fright, but I wasn't on a stage, only standing in a driveway looking at my beautiful daughters and yet not really knowing what to do. Thank the good Lord for a Mothers' instinct, as I gently said each one's name and hugged each, but felt as if my arms were around immovable objects, not humans. We did get past the initial entry and the many last minute preparations kept me busy and gave me time to regain my composure.

The wedding was a complete success and all said it was the most beautiful, in fact some said it was the closest to a royal wedding they had ever attended, and so it was, but to the family what was it really...a stepping stone to happiness or another hurt to add to the pain of life...only time would tell.

Ray and I often reflect on the riches in life as we so thought we had many as well as a close and loving family. We had planned all of our activities around our daughters, not only during their formative years but on into college and both Ray and I had attended every function. We denied the girls very little and attempted to add to their riches, the wealth that travel brings. All of my earnings that I acquired were put into a travel account so we could take one special trip a year and share the experience with our girls. We managed to visit almost every state in the Union, packing our station wagon not only to the brink inside, but also top loading it for sake of solving any problems of what to pack. Naturally each needed her own cases, her own entertainment etc., and while often "Barbie Dolls" filled the inside of the station wagon, the necessities were jammed on the top of the car. Nightly the girls would want their own suitcases so Ray would unload and accommodate. We always got a late start in the AM as each had to shower and shampoo before breakfast and all while Ray was loading up for the next stop. Thru it all he did very little complaining and we managed to drive from East to West and North to South. Only once do I recall him really loosing his cool and that is when the Barbie clothes managed to be thrown out the back window of the station wagon onto the highway as each was angry with her sister for one reason or another. Picking up Barbie clothes for a stretch of ¼ mile or so was not a fun adventure and for a day or so the car was very quiet with no Barbie's allowed on the scene.

Each trip was special and had a unique experience. One such trip was our "roughing it" in Yellowstone. The girls decided that would be the best so we stopped at an authentic Fishing Lodge where small fishing shacks were set up along a path leading to a lake. The group of cabins shared an outhouse, however, each one had its own pump. After touring the facilities the girls decided that the motel at the edge of Yellowstone Lake was as "rough" as they ever cared to go. In the Tetons we were able to "rough-it" in large floored tents complete with electricity, a large shared shower facility, swimming pool and breakfast cook-outs, so they did feel that their wishes had been granted. Panning for gold was fun in the cold streams until Darcy fell in and we decided enough of the outdoors for the Busch's although we did make a campfire and cook our evening meal outside before ending our nature outing.

Not all trips were quite as rustic, as we did take a wonderful train trip thru the Colorado Rockies and the Feather River Canyon en route to California. At the time Nancy was 5 and the others 11 and 12 respectfully. Our goal was to see the beautiful Redwood Forest, the California coastline and have the experience of the California Zephyr one-way and to fly home. The girls' goal was somewhat different than ours...theirs was to see movie stars and Disneyland and forget about the scenery. We managed to accomplish all, but not without difficulty as poor Debby was train sick for most of the time and the two nights and three days it took from Chicago to San Francisco was mostly spent in the bathroom for Debby and myself. The others used the Vistadome car for playing games, resting and reading, as we didn't get a sleeper because of the expense, but each girl had a pillow and blanket and a full seat in which to stretch-out with her gear.

When we arrived in San Francisco we rented a car and drove the beautiful drive from the Redwood Forests down the Monterey Coast and on to LA to see the stars and Disneyland. Our trip was almost ruined as our camera was stolen at Disneyland so we had to rent a camera, but never learned how to operate it, so our wonderful trip was never documented. The search for the Stars was something more difficult than we had expected. We took tours of their home areas, went to restaurants where they are "always seen" never to see anyone that even looked familiar. To the three older girls the trip was a waste until we got on the plane to fly back to Chicago and there on the same plane, but flying first class and not in the coach section as we were, was Bob Hope with his wife Delores. It was the highlight of our trip and once we landed he had his picture taken holding Nancy and flanked with the other three. We know why he is the super-star he is, so warm and compassionate for his fans. The girls were thrilled as they had seen and met a Super-star and had pictures to prove it to their friends.

Two years later we spent our vacation holiday in Hawaii as we wanted to show the girls Waikee and Honolulu over New Years. Our trip included visiting four Islands arriving at the Sheridan Waikee the day before New Years. We managed to get a suite on the top floor overlooking Diamond Head and Waikee Beach. It was a lavish suite with three rooms and two balconies, offered us for the same price as our modest paid accommodation which overlooked the parking lot, but which had been given by mistake to someone else. Never before had we known such luxury, but we graciously accepted our fate and enjoyed watching the fireworks in style. We also gave in to attending a rock concert in Diamond

Thrill of trip.
Bob Hope on our
American flight —
"Camera just for dogs."

Bob Hope, the Busch Idol loves his fans

Head featuring Santana on New Years Day, which was wild to say the least, but the girls all loved it, including Nancy. The girls had Hula lessons, attended a Luau and all on my salary as Wendy Ward. Mother would often tell us that we were foolish and should be saving for "old age", but Dad would chime in with the ever present sparkle in his eye and tell us to go and enjoy each and every trip as it was like a golden charm on a bracelet and every trip was an added charm to a golden memory. I have never forgotten that and know he was correct for I wouldn't change those memories for anything, and all of them I have on film, whether the old reel type or the new Video cassette...all except our trip to California.

Many of the vacations my folks shared, especially when the girls were very young and we would rent two cottages near Hayward, Wisconsin at a small lodge. Our entertainment was swimming in the lake, or playing cards in "Jack's" cabin, the name of the cabin we rented for two years. We would also drive into the small towns to see the Indians perform and it was wonderful being together. Blaisdell Lake Lodge was as fancy as we ever got with Mother and Dad and that had a dining room overlooking the lake. Mother especially liked this vacation, whereas Dad would prefer the rustic little "Jack" cabin eating scrambled eggs and playing cards with his "Little Honey", "Darling Doubles", and "Princess Shining Hair". He had such wonderful loving names for each and spent his entire time telling them wonderful original stories or playing little games with them.

Listing all the trips and going into any detail of each would be a book in itself, so to begin with the cabin trips with Mother and Dad and a trip to Mackinac Island when Nancy was only three months old and we rode bicycles with her in a basket seems a good place to start. Drives to the East to visit Washington, Williamsburg and the Historic monuments took one trip, while another took us to Florida and Disneyworld...a trip where the accommodations were paid for by Nancy when she was only four years old as this was part of her prize for winning the "Talented Tot" at a contest for pre-schoolers. The winner of the contest received three days lodging in Florida and so we drove down to pick up our winning lodging, not that the Motel ever expected to see us. The accommodations at the two-star Motel were not the greatest, but it was close to Disney World, which they all loved, as did we. All of our trips were via car, except to California and Hawaii, so we covered thousands of miles together and saw what each state had to offer. I'm so grateful now that we shared all these experiences with our girls and realize the wisdom that was Dad's, as each memory is golden.

Talented Tot Four-years-old 1966

The trip to Europe with Susan, Debby and Darcy as teenagers was mentioned earlier in the book in brief form, however I do think more of the details of the trip are now worth a few pages again. This was to visit the fashion capitals of the world and part of a promotional idea by Montgomery Ward to increase awareness of the Wendy Ward Program and Wards' interest in the fashion world. We visited London, Florence, Rome and Paris and the trip was fantastic in itself with experiences that could fill pages. Suffice it to say that London with its marvelous theaters and fashions was mind boggling to the teens. The excitement of

Piccadilly, Tower of London, Buckingham, Windsor Castle and seeing a Shakespearean production in Stratford on Avon were just a few of the highlights. The shopping at Harrods and seeing the private showing of "Twiggy" fashions was overwhelming and lastly the R production they saw entitled "Promises, Promises, which by today's standards would be mild as it was the play of which the movie version of "The Apartment" was taken. While I was viewing this with half of the teens on the tour as their chaperone, the remainder of the teens on the tour were seeing a nude production of Heloise and Abelaird. As chaperones we wondered what the repercussions would be when we returned to Chicago, but obviously none of the teen girls even mentioned the theater productions to their parents or if they did, it was acceptable, as long as the Wendy Ward Directors were there overseeing the event.

Florence and Rome proved to be most exciting as the Italians are such romantic fun loving people, and the men especially loved all the young American girls. I became somewhat of a "Mother Hen", keeping all of the young girls from harms way, avoiding any of the pinching, much to the girls' disappointment. In Rome we not only saw a private showing of the House of Pucci Fashions, but attended the Shakespearean Opera, "Aida" in the Baths of Caracalla across from the Coliseum. This was so awe inspiring to the teens as it was to the chaperones as well. Side trips to Assisi, Naples and Capri just added meaning and beauty to a most wonderful trip.

Paris was perhaps the most exciting with its wonderful Champs-Elysées and the Arch de Triomphe which is where we stood to watch the Bastille Day Parade and see DeGaulle riding in one of the hundreds of tanks in the procession. All the festivities with the House of Dior, Lancome and the various private showings that were showered on the fashion group of teens as well as all the wonderful special events whether a boat ride on the river Seine, or one of the Sound and Lights performances in each of the cities, or possibly the Follies Bergiere, all added up to an unbelievable trip for all there regardless, but especially for the teens as they were of such an impressionable age.

I really had my flying debut when Nancy was only 5 years old. Ray had been given the assignment from the University of Chicago to attend a Seminar in the Yucatan where he had some transactions to work on. I asked to go along, not stopping to think that this was to be my first flight and that I would not only be going alone, but on a foreign flight. All arrangements were made for me to join him and then he left for Mexico. After our good byes I realized that I would be on my own, not speaking the language, and that coupled with the fear of flying set up utter panic within me. My neighbor drove me to the airport and I remember asking at the International desk of Mexicana Airlines, when they inspected the suitcases for bombs at which they replied, "When we get there." Terrified I boarded the airliner and an understanding male flight attendant sat next to me and held my hand during take off. I must admit that once air-born I felt a feeling of relief as all my worrying was for naught, and to this day I enjoy flying, but shall never forget the terrible fear the first time.

Our trips have taken us all over the globe and we have now reached a point where we are visiting the more exotic and challenging countries. From the beginning of our many journeys Mother would remind us of our foolish spending, but I chose to remember the golden bracelet theory and still cling to that belief.

One of the first trips after our fiasco to Mexico was the forced holiday involving Susan's wedding, and although at the time I wasn't too excited about leaving Susan to plan the most important day of her life with Mike's Mother, the trip was a good idea and was very interesting and exciting. The Far East was different from any other place we had ever been and each and every place was wonderful. We started by taking the best flight we have ever had to date, that of JAL. It not only was a beautiful plane, but the service

Tram ride to the top of the world...Alps Switzerland

was unreal. We were given kimonos along with slippers to wear during our long flight. The food was excellent, and the flight attendants were really attending to our every whim, not only serving us, but keeping the airplane immaculate from take-off to landing, which is more than I can say about many planes we have taken in this country. Our stay in Tokyo was eye-opening as we experienced not only the cleanliness of the country, but the extreme patience of the people as they wait in long traffic jams without a horn honking or tempers flaring, as experienced everyday in Chicago. The management and staff also politely greeted us as we entered a large department store in the heart of Tokyo. Upon entering I noticed a camera hanging on a banister of the stairway by the jewelry department so upon telling this to the polite clerk behind the counter, she informed me that "yes, it had been hanging there for two days, but soon someone would come and get it". I couldn't help but think how long it would hang in any part of our country before being taken. Honesty and integrity seem to be their way of life and I felt renewed to meet people with such qualities. From Tokyo and Kyoto we bused to Hakone past Mt.

Fuji, which is usually hidden in the clouds. Although it was drizzling when we departed for Hakone, the clouds parted as we were approaching the beautiful Mt. Fuji and there it was in all its splendor. Many on the bus were in awe as the weather cleared up so suddenly, but somehow I had a feeling that it would as I always am a positive thinker and often it does pays off.

Attending New Year's Eve Royal Ball
Hapsburg Palace
Vienna, Austria 1986

Ruins with Nancy in Greece

Together enjoying the ruins, Nancy and I, 1984

From Spectacular to Spectacle,
Sharing fun with Nancy, 1984

School children – Beijing

Scenery spectacular - Hakone

From Japan it was Thailand with its beautiful palace adorned with precious jewels and gold that gleams so in the sunlight that you need sunglasses to peer at it for any length of time. The small river boats that took us on a cruise among the impoverished boat people of Bangkok opened our eyes and the small shacks built on stilts rose out of the polluted dark water to house a family with several children and at least one or two mange dogs as we peered into their tiny homes. When I asked about all the dogs I was told it was to keep away the snakes and rats that over-run the area. I was indeed impressed with all the poverty and yet the priceless objects of the Palace of the King of Siam...along with the many jeweled buildings belonging to the royalty. Never had I seen such a culture where the classes are so apparent and the squalor of Bangkok with the unpleasant aromas of the polluted water is a backdrop for immeasurable wealth. Only years later in India did I experience the same, but even more apparent.

Taiwan was a country that was special as there I perhaps stayed in my favorite hotel of all my travels. We upgraded on our own and stayed at the Grand Hotel, which sits on a hill overlooking the city. The gigantic columns of the front along with the monumental red Oriental gate flanking the hotel could be seen from the air and it looked like the Grand Hotel...red and magnificent as in the game of Monopoly. Upon our arrival there were honor guards and a red carpet rolled out for hundreds of feet for the King and Queen of Tonga who were arriving at any moment. We were perhaps ½ hour prior to their arrival and so were part of the massive audience lined up to receive the royalty and what an impressive couple...he must have weighed 400 lbs. wearing a colorful long robe and she must have weighed almost 300 lbs. What a wonderful additive to our first and only visit to Taiwan.

Singapore was equally interesting with their numerous laws on cleanliness as to littering, smoking etc., and although we were forewarned, one in our group did receive a $50.00 fine for smoking while walking on the sidewalk, and the group was held up until the fine was paid. The famous Raffles was as we had imagined from the film and we had to have a "Singapore Sling" while sitting in the large rattan fan chair. What seemed to impress me the most however was that we were driven via rickshaw thru the parks at 2:00 AM without worry about anyone or anything. Laws are very strict in the Orient and the crime rate is very low, a comfortable feeling when traveling. The country is beautiful, immaculate and there are flowers everywhere.

Our flight to Bali on Garuda Airlines turned out to be one of the highlights of our trip although we didn't realize it at the time. On board the small airlines I befriended an attendant, Annie Harriati, a beautiful Indonesian girl approximately 25 years old and as we talked most of the flight and she literally joined us when she wasn't serving others, I asked her if she had ever been anywhere but Indonesia. She was home-based in Jakarta and had spent her entire life there. I proceeded to invite her to visit us in Chicago if ever she could find a way to USA. Garuda airlines had reciprocity with KLM and she seemed interested. Weeks after we had returned to our home I heard from Annie and she said that her fiancé told her that Americans only talk and never mean what they say. With that I wrote back to inform her that indeed I did mean it and would welcome her to our home for a visit. Our plans were immediately put into high gear as we bought Ice Show tickets, and made arrangements to show a beautiful stranger a wonderful time. Much to our surprise when we met her at O'Hare she had two other flight attendants with her also to spend the week with us on their vacation, Trudy and Yuni, one more charming than the other. They assured us that they could all sleep in one bed and insisted when we arrived home. Without a doubt, they were the most charming guests we have ever had the pleasure of entertaining. Things we take for granted were new and exciting to these girls and the pleasures were mutual. They were rather poor by our standards and although they told me that they each brought "much money" with them, they each had about $100.00 equal to four months pay on Garuda Airlines. They each also had a rather long list of gifts they wanted to buy for their families. Thank goodness for Montgomery Wards at Randhurst and to Mel Pavlick, the manager as I called and told him of my dilemma and he informed me to shop in the "bargain basement" and that anything they wanted was immediately ½ sale for them that day. When Yuni had purchased 13 presents including a bra for her Mother, I felt that I now had bargain shopped for the first time. The bra size was determined only by asking a kind shopper what size she wore after explaining the situation...a strange question to be sure, but answered with sincerity. The Ice Show ended up with the three of them taking the good seats while Ray and I sat high up in the stands, not close enough to stop them at intermission from running down to the rink and bending down to feel and taste the ice. All in all it was a wonderful experience and this is after Mother always telling me to "never talk to strangers" had raised me The lesson is a good one, but some of the marvels of our trips have been because I do talk to strangers and mingle with the people.

Bali is perhaps one of the most beautiful, tranquil places I have ever visited. It must be what Hawaii was 200 tears ago. The Balinese girls are like beautiful dolls, so graceful and their nightly entertaining thru their costumed dancing left a memorable impression. Upon our arrival to Bali we were greeted with a colorful parade with people dancing, singing, papier-milch6 figures being carried including a huge bull being carried on a canopied platform. I asked if it was a holiday and was told no, it was a funeral and the entire town was celebrating the passing of a loved one on to Happy Land and that the body was in the Bull and the body and all were going to the ceremonial place to cremate all the food and special gifts would be sent with the loved one. I couldn't help but feel that maybe we are missing something to feel such suffering and pain when death approaches, when here it is entered into with such happy celebration. Makes me wonder what we really believe and why do we so dread funerals if we truly believe that there is a hereafter in a better place. I have experienced this in many cultures having traveled so extensively and still have not come up with any answers, but I must admit I to felt like celebrating with these sincere Balinese people.

The next year we took a month to go from Cape to Cairo on a planned tour. My love of animals and the desire to see them in their natural environment was the main focus of the trip. We began our tour in South Africa which was a marvelous experience starting with the Cape of Good Hope and its 10,000 species of wild flowers. Capetown, Johannesburg, and Durban were the main places we visited while in So. Africa, but each has a special meaning. In Johannesburg with all of its gold dumps and diamond mines I had decided to buy Nancy a beautiful ring and the others all gold. Nancy was the only one not married at the time so she always was the one to receive that little extra because she was the only one at home. The prices in Johannesburg were very high and when I found the ring of my choice for Nancy, I saw for the first time that Ray really wanted me to have a the best first and although I was not used to spending a lot on myself, but more on my family and for our home, he insisted on buying me a beautiful golden nugget with a diamond attached. He said if he couldn't buy it for me then I couldn't buy the ring for Nancy. Although I did feel it was extravagant it is now one of my favorite pieces of jewelry.

From Durban with its crashing surf, supposedly one of the largest surfs in the world we went on to Zimbabwe and to Victoria Falls, one of the most spectacular sights I've ever seen. Before going to Victoria Falls we flew into Salisbury, Rhodesia, which was in turmoil with military everywhere and the tension, was very strong. We were told not to leave our hotel for the evening and as we left the next morning a coup was about to happen with brick and bottles being thrown. Needless to say we were glad to board the plane and leave for Victoria Falls and the Victoria Falls Hotel situated on the edge of the Falls and the rain forest and it was absolutely magnificent. The roar of the Falls was so deafening that one had to shout to be heard, and the spray of the gigantic falls could be felt from the grounds of the Hotel. We left and continued on to Kenya only to hear that five days after we left the hotel the rebels and taken it over and killed several tourists...again a near miss, but thank God a miss.

Our first stop in Kenya was the Mount Kenya Safari owned by Bill Holden, a posh resort in the heart of Africa, not home to wild animals as I had imagined, but to beautiful birds such as Peacocks, many white Peacocks, and beautiful colorful birds. The grounds were manicured and private cottages as well as the main lodge was set with the Kenya Mts. as a back-drop. Although it was fantastic it was not what I would choose for my habitat in Africa; however, the next stop at the Tree Tops was as rugged as I have stayed in, stationed over a watering hole as an Oasis for hundreds of wild animals, was enchanting. I managed to obtain a seat directly over the watering hole on the second level and literally stayed there for over 24 hours to watch the most wonderful show on earth taking place before my eyes as we saw and heard the Wildabeasts coming and going all night with the cries of the Hyenas coming out of the shadows to attempt to lure one of the baby Wildabeasts away. The large Bull Wildabeasts would charge the Hyenas back into the darkness. Through all of this the little wart hogs with their bent front legs were running around and playing among the Wildabeasts, and in the distance the sounds of the Elephants. I have never experienced anything quite like this and the emotions that I felt as I viewed this ever changing site were overcoming. In the early AM the sunrise over the Kenya Mts. rounded out a natural beauty that I had never before experienced.

Thinking that nothing could ever surpass what I had seen we headed to Amboselli Lodge deep in the heart of Kenya where we went on early morning runs in our six person jeep. Amboselli is opposite Mt. Kilimanjaro and the view is awesome. Our small cabins had bars on the windows and mosquito netting around our beds, and we were told to keep our doors closed at all times. One tourist forgot and came back from a Safari to find her clothes all strung from the tops of the tall trees by the native monkeys and baboons. When we left Amboselli her clothes were still there and made for great filming. The runs were very exciting, however, I was concerned that I might witness a kill. Thankful that we never saw a kill, only a feeding of two lionesses and their young on an already killed Wildabeast, gave me some relief. The male lion was hanging from a tree waiting for the females and the young to eat before he would take his turn. I very soon realized that this is the law of nature as I saw bones picked absolutely clean by each in turn as others finish and the vultures have the final take. No waste, only survival and this I could handle.

While in Kenya we learned of Sadat's assassination and while many tour members opted not to go on to Cairo, we had our course planned and never deviated. The size and mystique of the ancient monuments were beyond our imagination and we knew the decision to continue on had been the right one. Our trip to Karnak and the Valley of the Kings was one we shall never forget as we climbed the narrow steps to King Tutankhamen's tomb buried in the sands. Centuries of grandeur buried with the elaborate tomb and the sarcophagus of the famous King. We also climbed the pyramid of Aesop, rode camels and marveled at the magnificent Sphinx both during the days trip by camel to the Sphinx, and at night to the awesome production of "Sound and Lights" at the Sphinx.

Europe had been a choice of our four trips, each to different locations and each adding new dimensions to our travel journal. The scenic beauty of Switzerland and Austria, the fun loving people of Italy with the nostalgia that comes from riding in a gondola or eating in a small sidewalk café, the magnificent monuments and cathedrals in Spain, France, Greece and England. In each and everyplace we travel I see the need to help stray animals and although I often wish I could ignore the helpless creatures, I never can. In Greece I saw a donkey tied in the hot sun, no water, and wearing a colorful blanket while being rented out for short rides. I immediately got off the tour bus and after a $5.00 donation I had the man move and tie his donkey in the shade along with a pail of water while the others on the bus all cheered. I attempted to explain to the donkey owner that Americans are very concerned about care of animals and would never hire from a non-caring person and he told me that he wanted to please tourists and in the future he would be concerned about the donkey. I may have accomplished nothing, but if I helped one poor donkey it was worth my small effort.

On tours food is always abundant and so I have learned to carry a large plastic bag to every meal so that I can fill it with our scraps and extra bread if a buffet, as well as extra food I can put on my plate. Others on cruises have asked me what I am doing and often I see others also clearing plates and asking for seconds to put in their bag and later feeding the strays.

During Nancy's senior year in College we joined her in a political Science tour to the Soviet Union for one month during her winter term. The College needed two more students to get the study group tour off the ground so we signed on as "older students" and off we all went to Russia, total cost per person including airfare, all entertainment including the Bolshoi Ballet, numerous circuses and ballets, all room and board was only $1,400.00 each. Never have we had such an economical trip before since it was for one month, but the month was January and the temperature in the Soviet Union was in minus digits and not calculated with wind chill factors as we do in Chicago. Our coldest was in Leningrad where the temperature read 32 below zero with the winds whipping off the Bay of Finland. Moscow was not much warmer but the experience was worth any inconvenience. It was a trip of a lifetime and I learned that if given the chance people are people, loving and caring. This seems to be true everyplace we go and all they need to know is that we are their friends and the response is awesome. I left with a group of skeptics, including my husband who was

Winter term in Soviet Union, Uzbeckestan

certain that the KGB would be following our every move. Dr. Raymond, the Political Science Professor at DePauw spoke fluent Russian as he had conducted several other winter terns to Russia. Upon arrival in Moscow I felt a coldness, not only from the temperature, but from the Russian people as they looked down when you approached them. I wrote as such on a postcard to my Mother that evening and told her of my observation. Ray was convinced that she would never receive the card, which she did. The next day the entire group was invited to attend a Russian Seminar on life and living in Russia and of the entire tour I was the only one to attend. All, including the professor were sure it was to be all propaganda, but it was far from that. The large room held many tourists from around the world and three Communist party members sat on the stage and told us what we might expect and why and then also answered questions. The older woman remarked about the incorrect surveillance we might have of the people appearing unfriendly, but in fact that is just the opposite...that they

wait for the first overture from foreigners and that if we would
only smile at a group of Russians we would see their true feelings.
She also pointed out the lack of quality that the Soviets possess in
the manufactured goods. She said they were the largest shoe
manufacturer in the world, but the quality is so bad that the boots
last only a few months and that Russia could learn much from their
"Western Neighbors." I must say that didn't sound like propaganda
to me nor did the remainder of the program. When the lecture was
over I raced outside to try the experiment of presenting a friendly
overture to the people that felt somewhat inferior by their dress,
their inability to travel as they have only rubles not recognized
outside the Iron Curtain, and the many other incidentals pointed
out at the seminar. Needless to say, my smile was received by hugs
and handshakes and the placing of lapel pins on my coat as they
hugged me and said "friend". It brought tears to my eyes to see
these warm loving persons so misunderstood by arrogant persons
such as the college group I was traveling with, including my
husband, that refused to give strangers a chance, but would rather
sit and agree to chastise persons they are not willing to meet
halfway. I was able to convince my husband to attend a seminar at
the next stop and he saw for himself exactly what I told him, that
there was no propaganda, only people in leadership positions
attempting to explain to travelers their way of life. In this
particular seminar we arrived a little late and had missed the hand-
outs, so after the meeting they asked for our name and address in
America and sent to us in Chicago several bound beautiful books
of Russia and the Soviet Union. I wonder what we would have
done for our foreign visitors who were late for a meeting. I'm truly
convinced as I travel throughout the world that the only
propaganda comes from the governments such as ours and so many
Americans are "ugly Americans" as they are so pampered and
spoiled in the extravagant lifestyle we enjoy in America that they
put on blinders and think that everyone else is not only beneath us,
but should do as we do and live up to our standards. Ray too
started to notice the sincerity of the people and was amazed at their
generosity and caring attitude. While growing up Mother always

emphasized that I should never talk to strangers, and while a child or a teen that is perhaps good advice, but as an adult I find the only way to really enjoy and understand people is thru communication, if not with words, then with eyes or hand gestures, or pictures if at all possible. I have been able to communicate with persons all over the world and with no difficulty and yet only speak English. One such time was in Russia when Ray and I decided to take the Metro around Moscow and sat opposite a young man holding a violin case. He was rather shabbily dressed by our standards, but our eyes met and thru gestures I told him that I loved the violin and played it myself. He then offered us tickets to come to see the concert he was performing in and when we indicated we were on a tour and couldn't come, he asked if we wanted to come to a rehearsal and once again we had to refuse. At that point he wanted to know where we were staying in Moscow and our name so we told him. Several hours later we returned to our hotel to find a little box in our mailbox from "your friend, the violinist", a little black lacquered pin with a flower painted on it and I cried. Imagine this young man going across town to leave a friendly token to a stranger that had spent ten precious minutes with him on a train in Moscow. My heart is full when I think of people like this and I realize that the world is so full of goodness with loving people around that I find traveling a real humbling experience, that thru this journal I hope to relate to my daughters, their families and to anyone else who reads this. I could go on and on with examples of love among strangers, but only a few more shall I put into print and one was in Uzbekistan when we stayed in Somerkand for several days. Ray had decided to take a side trip to another small republic of the Soviet Union and I decided to take my video, which I always carried with me, my bag of bread for any stray animals I saw, and I wandered off to the more residential part of Somerkand. Our hotel was located across the street from a park and everyday I would go across the street with my bag of goodies and feed the stray dogs that lived under the streets in the culverts.

The people sitting in the park would smile, clap and show a

thumbs up sign to me when the dogs would come out from the culvert, wag their tails and eat. I never attempted to pet any stray, only feed them, and maybe I left the Soviet people with the idea to love and take care of the strays after I left...if so, then I did accomplish a lot.

My day on the day in question led me to a small residential area that was somewhat crowded with quanset type dwellings. As I walked along I saw curious glances, but only nodded and smiled. On a corner I came upon a corner grocery store, a tiny establishment with both an older man and woman sitting on stools as I entered. The selection was very limited, but I did notice beautiful cigarette packages on a shelf. Some were decorated with Troykas, others with Russian Wolf-hound dogs, so I decided to purchase some of these for the packaging only to display in our recreation room at home. Upon pointing out the packages I wanted, I noticed their curiosity so I smiled and gestured that I was Mama and did not smoke, only Papa smokes. They understood immediately and the woman took me by the hand to a candy barrel, took out several wrapped candies and put them in my pocket and said "Mama" and pointed to the candy and said "Papa" and pointed to the cigarettes. She then ran to the door and called to neighbors who came running and soon the store was filled with possibly 15 to 18 persons and she was telling them how I ate candy and Papa smoked. It was one of the most delightful afternoons...all hugged me good-bye and stood outside waving as I left feeling warm and good inside.

China was vast and so unlike any other encounter, was one that really was an eye-opener. Our trips have now all taken over one month duration to really see the areas and cultures, as well as mingle with the people as best we can. Our tour included visiting Shanghai, Beijing, Chunking, and many other large cities in China as well as a wonderful Yangtze Cruise which was unforgettable. The Yangtze is unlike any body of water I had ever seen, swirling and treacherous, mud-brown in color and often a cow or possible a human has been caught in the fast moving current that swirls past. Although the scenery was beautiful, the turbulent waters were anything but relaxing. The cruise ship itself was very small, held about 60-80 passengers and had none of the amenities that we associate with Cruise ships. While on the cruise Ray had a birthday and I decided to surprise him with a cake and a full day with the masseur. In this case the masseur was the barber, the beautician and manicurist and had been so for over 40 years on the same little ship. I arranged for him to come to the cabin and give Ray a massage after which he would take him to the barbershop, give him a head and scalp massage and then cut his hair. I also arranged with the ships "cruise director", who was one of the few who spoke English, was also the purser and who made all announcements on ship. I told him I should like to order a birthday cake for my husband and he asked if I wanted the "ships' free cake" or did I want to pay for it. I decided to be most frugal and told him I would take the "ship's free surprise birthday cake", after which he made an intercom announcement inviting everyone to "Mr. Busch's Free Ship's Birthday cake surprise party after supper." I loved it, the simplicity and honesty of this wonderful Chinese man attempting to understand and please. The masseur was equally unforgettable as he came to the cabin and proceeded to kneed, chop, twist and pinch every muscle as well as crack every joint, and all while Ray held onto the mattress grimacing. After a lengthy session of torture he followed the little Chinese man into the barber shop while I videotaped more treatments. During the entire session the Chinese man never said a word nor changed his expression. When he finished with a scalp and neck massage he began the hair cut which was not a style chosen by Ray nor me, as I was too busy taking videos, however, it was an Oriental style much like the barbers, shaved high above the ears with a flat top and although Ray was far from happy, his hair did eventually grow back and the experience was one he shall never forget, and all for a total charge of $7.00. On our trip to China I experienced one of the most moving and most memorable times of my life. It was on our way back from viewing the ancient Buddhist carvings recently uncovered in the mountains which had just opened to the public. Our tour guide as well as our bus driver did not want to, but the entire tour voted to go as it was optional in the brochure. The temperature was well over 100 degrees and the roads were terrible, full of ruts without much of a visible road at all. After visiting the excavated site our bus hit the ruts and blew two tires. We were somewhere between Wuhan and Wangoo in territory probably not visited by many white men and with no shelter save a few little trees. In the fields were Chinese farmers hand-hoeing their crops, both men and women with babies on their backs. The driver hitched a ride with a coal truck and left to go for help and the other tourists headed for the few shade trees to help them with the extreme heat. I, however, suggested to Ray, "Let's sing for the Chinese farmers," so we stood in the middle of the dirt road singing anything that came to mind from 'God Bless America', to 'Jingle Bells' and 'Deep In The Heart of Texas'. As we sang the farmers left their fields and came over surrounding us, and as we stopped they clapped, smiled and fanned us with little hand-woven straw fans. We not only sang to them, but showed them ballroom dancing from slow waltzing to our own vocal accompaniment to jitter-bugging to 'Boogie Woogie Bugle Boy'. The heat was extreme but the Chinese farmers were so very excited, clapping, fanning, and smiling and to us to stop was not in our thought at all. Finally I decided how much fun to teach them an American game such as 'London Bridge'. Ray and I demonstrated by holding our hands in the air making the bridge and singing, but no farmer would go under our hands so we finally put two Chinese ladies hands together and Ray and I continued to bend down and go under while singing. For me it wasn't difficult, but at 6'1" and in 100 degree heat it was extremely difficult for Ray. After 3½ hours of singing, dancing and playing games the bus was fixed and ready to go and all of a sudden the women with babies who had always stood in the back of the crowd and somewhat shielded their babies from us now stepped up to me and held out their infants to me. The moment was so electrifying, so emotional, as here were people with nothing but their babies, now wanting me to know they trusted me and liked me. I held each baby in my arms and cried as I did and sang "Rock-a-bye Baby" to each. Everyone on the bus was also crying and I shall never forget the experience as I kissed each little baby on the head. It was to me a moment of truth unspoken, a feeling so deep within by persons unable to communicate with words, but only with love and trust. My Father was so right when he said to travel and see the world, that each trip would be a memorable charm on a golden bracelet of life and that's what they have been. Each has had its place in our memorabilia and we have set one room in our home filled with only travel treasures from every corner of the world. To visitors it is a most interesting room filled with African artifacts, an Australian filled cabinet with Aborigine art, a section of Far East treasures, not expensive, but to us, irreplaceable. It is our haven where we sit and watch our wonderful movies and videos from around the world and where we escape the everyday pressures and relive our wonderful experiences.

Most of our early trips we were able to share with both Mother and Dad as we always took movies, had scrap books, and many tales to tell and while Mother only seemed relieved that we had returned safely, Dad was most eager to listen to every detail. He could envision each and every story as he had been my Master teacher and had taught me to embellish thoughts with detail and in descriptive terms. How I wanted to spend more time with Dad and learn from his wisdom and years of knowledge. My desire to be nearer him and to include Mother and Dad in our daily lives started me wondering about the possibility of having them move to Mount Prospect in their own little home near us. I knew Mother had always disliked her home in Eau Claire and longed for a home on a quiet street, a home with a view of something other than traffic, and since they were now past retiring age I decided to look and see what was available knowing that their finances were limited so Ray and I would have to assist in this undertaking. I began shopping for the perfect small home unbeknown to them. After months I found what I thought to be the perfect home...a small ranch on a corner lot, surrounded with a picket fence and a small yard for Mother's garden and for Dad to feed the birds and enjoy his love of the outdoors. It was within walking distance to the little shops of Mount Prospect and Dad did so like to walk and talk to people, and yet the street was very quiet with lovely tall trees lining both sides of the street. My excitement grew and I talked to the owner, a widow, who kindly showed me the home priced at $50,000. I believed this was doable with our help and so with enthusiasm discussed the idea with Ray who agreed that if I continued to work and we cut down on our yearly trips we could indeed help.

For You Daughter

HAPPY BIRTHDAY WITH LOVE

down-Mother

I think she is

eel)   ; So

mething done

e immediate wo

takes us dee

8the life we l

ght say is "the

sun and the co

- somehow wit!

with me into tl

a busy little

ring over to

*From Him from
whom all Blessings
come

I have a
Daughter.*

y existence= May my heart beat. ...

t "runneth over"   and say to you as we sit here=close each

the other-You my daughter -have made it "All worth while "-

ill I ever feel that whatever of little effort I may have put i

ls thing called life-has not been fully paid-becase of YOU. .

ve to my darlings-Wards will repair the clos ~~RD~~ *Love Ford*

Reason for living... Love Dad

137

Eau Claire Wisconsin.

Jenese Dear:

It has been my priviledge to spend the week end with
the finest people I know- From the moment we saw you standing ourside
until we told and waved Good Bye- every moment-every expression bespoke
a welcome that only a lovin, family could give. From the tender gestures
of my little Princess Shining Hair- and the sweet companionship of the
girls- I read a welcome that only real affection can evidence. I too
enjoyed the discussions with Ray-it is not my priviledge to often talk with
so interest a a person.
But now to you my daughter- this is close to our understanding each
of the other-I know-though at your home I did not want to appear to
be outspoken on this- - how many little things you did for me-for me
alone-just the little things that so clearly say" for you Dad"-things
that might go un-noticed-that are of the moment-yet-I so need someone
to say it in the way you did- - I find noefault with life -every day is
kind to me-every day brings to me duties and obligations which in themselves
are rewarding-yet-somehow-when I recall the sweetness that permeated
everymoment with you-there is a satisfaction that only understanding
reached out and says" take of me your fullest needs-quaff deep because
this moment is not for ever- take of it and remember"
And my Daughter <u>remember I shall</u>- --there is so much to enjoy in the
"Remembering" For the love that each of your little CLAN showed to me
-I am grateful- for he tenderness I briefly knew-I am appreciative --
for the companionship I enjoyed-I am hungering-BUT most of each
hour since I left for home- I have held close to my heart the the
knowledge that only MY ONLY DAUGHTER could tell me in so many wonderful
ways-that she is still "Heart of my heart "
                                        Your Dad

Letter from Dad

At Home;

Jenese Dear:

This is not intended to be a letter—it is not to tell you how rainy and stormy the weather was all the way back home nor is it to convey to Mother how very lonely the house was—in every nook and corner when I came in. Rather it is —if you will—a sort of visit with myself— a soliloquy—a summing up of this thing called life as I know it and live it— the piecing together of that fabric that makes a day —something of a number of moments added together— each with its own action—its own memory—its own livability and treasure—and as I am here in my lonliness and thoughts I find myself asking HIM to help me say a word of gratitude and great thankfulness for what He has given to me— I live now again that moment when as on our visit to your home— you put your arms around me and said "Hello Dad" and Ray's handshake —the warmth of that bit of affection that makes a moment —just a passing nothing or a treasured memory to last a life Time— but even more—yes —a greater gift was mine as each of my loved ones—in sweet childhood manner bespoke that deep " affection" that only a child's unassuming honesty can make "real" and reach beyond the outer smile and word and into the heart of him who may be the object of that gesture. And so—my daughter—may HE give to us the recipient of all of that love— the power to fully appreciate such gifts as it is granted t o very few to know and cherish—and when I have asked you to accept my humble thanks for the happy hours you have made possible to me— through your children's love and affection— I — I find that you are now repaying the love a Father gave to his only daughter when s h e was his " Little Punkie". Tell Little Darcy a special wish goes with this for her t o get well,

Love

Dad.

Eau Claire Wisconsin.

Jemese Dear:

      I want to thank you for the wonderful thought you
have shown to me for father's day- first for the nice and beautiful gift
that has so much of ~~XXXXXXXXXXX~~ usefulness built into it- and then for that gift whic h
some hears ago you promised-all unknowingly to share with me-and so
after talking with you Sunday-I went slowly to my room-quietly closed
the door and there on the velvet back drop of memories-gently laid
out the beauty of your life's gifts to me- I must look carefully for
time has mayhap blurred a little the vision of that baby stare or was it
a baby grimade that I first saw as the nurse gently placed in my arms that
bit of humanity that was to be=for me-soemthing of life itself--and now-
along life's rrail we travel together you and I- the first scary day at
kindergarten- my then waiting anxiously for school to let out so that
i might take you home-the first day you had been away from us for maybe
three or four hours- and then the process of growing up- the compptetition
for the playground swings-Dad to the rescue with a bag of candy- then
here and there throughout t e problems of study and companions- you
and I-always your problems and difficulties-mine-to try and understand and
share. Amd so through High school and college-and as you moved along life's
pathway=even though you were away from my side -you were closer than
before -because we -though you were always my FUNKIE-you were still
a woman- and with the burdens that somehow or other we all must meet-
you at times needed me- and May I now f eel that I have been for you as
the necessities of the moment measured me. In your presne t glory as a
beloved wife and Mother I find my life being fulfilled- I know too-w th
my daughter the tenderness o that moment when first-my baby daughter was
neing placed in my arms and in my heart. and so-my Dear-I humbly thank
the Almight God -and you for a
          WONDERFUL FATHERS DAY.
                  Love DAD.

Eau Claire Wisconsin.

My Daughter:
          I speak now along to you.
  In thought I am beside you while man's inventive genius speeds you across
thousands of miles of space in less time than the sun does take to
sink to rest in the west and rise again in the east. Silently I glory in
the luxuries provided for you-- the wonderful conveniences-the
tastiest of foods-then the glory of the dazzling lights-   the ocean
beaches-and you-with that child -like wonder in your eyes as each
new magnificence unfolds for you-this do I thrill with as I see it thrill
you.--- and here we hesitate- a beautifully gowned -dazzling young matron
lifts a jar of flowers from a table-removes the flowers-and insists
that the glass be filled with milk-that a bag of food be furnished-
(now must I rub my eyes)-no-not I -your father- for as my daughter
you could do no less. And with what of life is left- a poor little
scrawny tail wags in gratitude -and brown eyes look up--and I know

          The chimes of heaven peal softly earthward in recognition
          that in this busy selfish , conceited world of man there still
          beats a heart that can know compassion for a helpless-homeless
          puppy.

          And so I take your hand in mine and whisper to you my daughter-
          The sun should be a diadem in your hair
          And you should have the moon and stars to wear;
                         "were mine the choice"
               God bless you.
                         Love

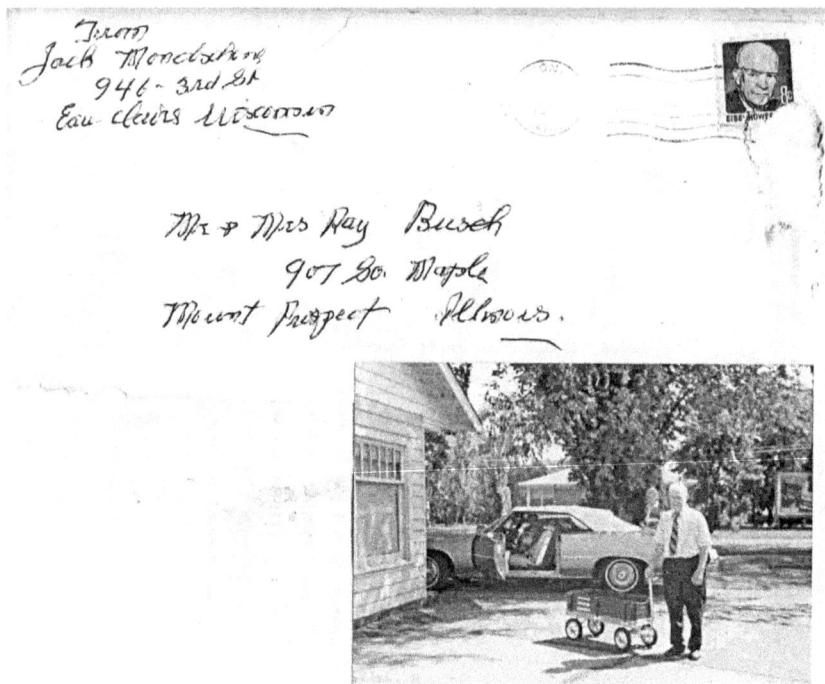

Envelope and note from Dad

With all plans in place and every aspect well thought out I eagerly awaited our soon to be visit to Eau Claire. The year was 1974 and the winter snows had all disappeared as it was now spring and everything promised a new beginning, a re-awakening, and so the scene was set as we drove to Eau Claire. Every other time our visits had evolved around the girls, their activities and our own special pleasures. This time would be different. I had always wanted the best for Mother and Dad as they had worked so hard all during my years in Eau Claire and now I was an adult with four daughters, a husband who was an attorney, and I was working for entertainment and trips. I had suddenly realized we had so much and now I could finally give something back and help my dear parents. Mother's dream had always been a small home with a view, on a quiet street, and now I had found just that. As we drove into the driveway of the station next to the large yellow house where two anxious parents were awaiting our arrival, I could hardly contain myself I suggested to Ray that I walk alone with Dad along our banks of the Chippewa River and he would visit with Mother while she prepared our dinner. Never did I realize at the time that this would be the last time I would ever walk the path we had taken for so many years, that the rough, knurled hands I held I would never hold again, but I do thank God for giving us this last time together. It perhaps was the most memorable day of my life as Dad and I sat holding hands in the shade overlooking our beloved river. I told him of my idea, that now I could help he and Mother so they could enjoy their life in Mother's dream house near us. I babbled on and on in excitement, of how I could afford to help them now, when suddenly the world stood still as Dad held both of my hands in his and looked into my eyes. He spoke softly and the words still ring in my ears 24 years later, "My Dearest Little One, my precious Jenese...you're so very, very special, but it's time you knew something and then we'll talk later." I had never seen such a pensive look on his face as he searched for the proper words to say. "You see my little darling, I don't need your money. There isn't any home in Eau Claire that your Father couldn't buy and pay cash for," and then he paused. "I know my dearest one that someday you will understand." I had never questioned my Father's statements in all my life he has always told me the truth, but what was he saying to me now? He no longer wanted to discuss anymore details, but said we'd talk again and again, and also told me that he did want me to me a promise, as he took both hands in his and looked into my eyes, which were now flooded with tears. "My Darling Daughter, promise me that if anything should ever happen to me that you will take the necessary money available and buy your Mother her dream house." After I promised faithfully to do so, but also said I didn't want him to talk like that, he also told me that "you have married an honorable man who will take good care of you and the children and someday both you and Ray will be very proud of him and by now I was sobbing and told him I had always been proud of him and he never had to prove himself to me. Had I known this would be our last time to sit and hold hands, or listen to the water rushing over the rocks or the birds singing in their many tones I should have never let go of his hand or stopped him from pouring out his heart to me but he seemed to want to continue at a later date and let me absorb what he had said, preparing us for the next time. Never before had he talked to me in such a way, never had he revealed any dark kept secrets, only this time, but why now. Had I changed enough to have my Father take me into his confidence or did my deep show of caring and concern for Mother and Dad's life bring this about? Had he always waited for me to show him a sign or signal that he could now open a door to the past or maybe to the future? All the many mysteries of my Father, this wonderful man haunted me for sometime until the truth was all revealed to me thru the finding in one small trunk.

On a drive back to Mount Prospect I eagerly and yet hesitantly told Ray about my Father's and my conversation. Hesitant because we differed so in our sensitivities, but yet I had to talk about it. I told Ray what Dad had said about being able to purchase any home in Eau Claire and pay cash for it, and about this statement that "someday I'll make you and Ray proud of me", as if I hadn't been proud of Dad for 45 Years of my life. Ray reminded me of Dad's ability to tell stories, wonderful fairy tale to the children that he had a gift for being creative and I was totally mistaken if I thought Dad had any money. He pointed out so many things I already knew...how Mother had worked in a factory for years and how before she had taken in neighborhood washing. He also reminded me that we really lived in a modest duplex on the poorer side of Eau Claire...how he had but one pair of shoes, resoled until the leather no longer held out...how he drove an old panel car on which he did all his own oil and grease jobs. He kept going on and on reminding me that when I was in desperate need after the divorce he offered no money, only compassion and guidance. All what he said was true and yet in my heart I knew that Dad had money and had tried to tell me so, but I couldn't answer all the unanswered questions on why, when or where, but then I had never questioned Dad on anything and now I knew that our next visit together many unanswered question would get answered. Today was only to open the door a crack, but the next time...

There never was a next time as Dad died on October 24, 1974 at 4:30 in the afternoon. I know because it was Sunday. I had spoken to them on the phone earlier and Dad was planning to watch the Vikings play football while Mother prepared a little lunch for the two of them. At 4:30 I got a terrible chill and started to shake...I had never had such a sinking feeling, which lasted a short time and I attributed it to the flu although it came and left so quickly. Shortly after the phone rang and it was Mother. She was hysterical, screaming, and crying and thru it all I heard the words, "Jenese...come quickly...your Father is dead." How could that be as only a few hours earlier we had such a cheerful happy visit on the phone.

I left on the next plane to Eau Claire. I don't remember making any arrangements, only that I needed to go alone and right away and so I did. When the plane landed in Eau Claire, my Mother's neighbor Louie Coyer was there to pick me up and drive me to our home. Mother was there and sobbing while neighbors were attempting to console her. When she saw me she clung to me as if I had to hold her up as well as myself And although my heart was breaking I was so strong, stronger than I ever knew I could be. Dad had always taught me that "we are tuffies and can face anything with courage" so now my inner strength took over. Mother and I cried together for sometime and she told me how Dad had watched part of the Viking game, but decided during half time to go for a walk by the river. While walking he was seen by the neighbors to stoop over to pet a dog no one knew whose dog, possible a stray, but while petting the dog he toppled over with a heart attack. How fitting that he should go in such a way, as he loved animals so and

to me had always been my "St. Frances of Assisi". His last words
to Mother as he went out the door were, "I'll be back shortly."

I stayed in Eau Claire and made all the arrangements for a
wake at the Funeral Home located across from the Chippewa
River. It somehow seemed fitting and proper. I also made
arrangements to fly Dad back to Mount Prospect with me so I
could bury him near us. Ray was wonderful on the Mount Prospect
scene. He arranged with Larry Hinkelmana at the Methodist
church to have a small service and he also purchased a four-grave
sit in Ridgewood Cemetery where his Father is buried, a beautiful
location, as I told him it had to be under a big tree with four
together, and so it is. The site is located under a large Oak Tree
and across from a pond where there are Swans and
Ducks...everything happened so quickly and I kept going so
everything would be perfect for Dad and also easier for Mother.
She had completely fallen apart and could do nothing...and I saw a
frightened very weak, almost a young child, completely dependant
and scared to face life alone. I had never seen open devotion for
Dad before, but now she seemed unable to let go. I did have a few
private moments with my Father at the funeral home and he looked
so peaceful and beautiful, wearing his only suit...the one he wore
when we danced, the night I was Prom Queen...so many flash-
backs, and alone with Dad I held onto every memory and relived
every moment I had had with my wonderful Father. From him I
got my strength, my courage, my sensitivities, my memory my
willingness to thrive on, my ability to lead and take care of my
family, and my great love for animals. I felt such a weight on my
shoulders but I knew my role in life was now a protector and giver
and not anymore to be protected and take. In an instant I was no
longer the "little Punkie" but would always be Jenese Darling."

Ray and the girls drove Mother back to Mount Prospect after
the wake as I flew back with Dad. How often I had wanted to fly
with Dad, but not like this. I really had wanted to fly with Dad to

Istanbul to see his famous legacy embossed in bronze in a museum, "I wept because I had no shoes and then I saw a man who had no feet." I would have flown anywhere with Dad, but never encouraged it too much as he always seemed hesitant, but now we were together but in separate parts of the plane. The hearse was at the airport and Dad was taken directly to the small church on Gulf Road in Arlington Heights.

It was a very small audience, only immediate families and Ray's family all except Carl who wouldn't attend because funerals upset him. I resented his attitude but only told Ray of my feelings. For only one moment did I again have a sinking feeling and that is when I left him alone at Ridgewood Cemetery, but the feelings left as I returned often to sit in the shade of the tree and talk to Dad after kissing the bronze head-stone on both sides, like he always kissed me on both cheeks. The marker is a beautiful bronze, etched and embossed with oak leaves and acorns and inscribed by a most beautiful verse written by Debby at 18 years of age.

"The journey of a tattered newsboy with naught in life but a will...
to reach the highest mountain rather than climb the hill...
He chose to look thru poet's eyes and look to him above...
The one who gave us on his way, his precious gift of love"
Debby Busch 10/28/74

How inspiring as she too had the sensitivities and creativeness of my Father and summed up his life so beautifully.

After the funeral Mother remained in Mount Prospect for approximately one week but was restless to go back so I drove her to Eau Claire to help and comfort her. First I had to remove all of Dad's things all the merchandise upstairs, in the basement and in the station. With the help of her two best friends, Rose Sherman and Ione DuBois kept Mother occupied at their homes. I also contacted several customers of Dad's and obtained the names of his chief competitors as manufacturers representatives. I brought in the salesmen and offered the entire stock to the highest bidder. All must be purchased and removed by highest bidder. I became the bargaining tool for a nice sum to use for the home in Eau Claire...to make it comfortable and a new look for Mother, as she no longer wanted to leave the home. First to go was the filling station and in its place a small sun-porch. Service Master cleaned everything including coal-bin, after which entire interior of home painted in sofa natural tones. Pale plush green carpet covered all floors on first floor while wood floors upstairs were cleaned and polished.

It was while working on the upstairs where Dad had kept most of his merchandise that the small trunk was found in a small crawl space never before noticed. I never even knew the space existed nor had Mother. The trunk has opened a whole New World to me...an insight into my Father, and the answers to so many unanswered questions. Shocked and speechless I started to go thru each precious memorabilia Dad had saved over the years. I discovered letters written to my Father from his Mother urging him to return to the temple and Dad's Jewish heritage. Why was I never told I was of Jewish heritage? There was also documentation that my Father Jack David Mondschine born around 1900 was really Israel David Mondschine born in 1886. It was all there...his report cards...his library card issued in 1901 in Duluth, Minnesota, along with all of these documents were so many of his original manuscripts. There were also documents and some gold piece that went back to Napoleon's time. I to date have no idea of the worth of the coins; however I did find several Abraham Lincoln memorabilia including a program to the Ford Theater playing the "Cousins" program the night Lincoln was assassinated, and it was signed Fannie Mondschine's program. This I now have framed along with an old "Springfield Gazette" clipping referring to Abe Lincoln's' opening of his first law office, but it states "he will still shod horses and mend fences." Abe Lincoln had been my Father's idol and he had saved many memorabilia from 1865.

Finding the trunk and all the surprises I decided to attempt to see what if any money Dad had as none was found. The bank in Eau Claire revealed a rather large lock box and so with proper documents, an officer of the bank and Ray, as I had asked him to be there also, we opened the lock box and shock and amazement took over as we found over $1,000,000.00 worth of Stocks and Bonds. The shock of such wealth was overwhelming and amidst tears and disbelief we listed and itemized each stock and bond as well as all assets. Ray was stunned, unable to speak, and the back officer shared in the amazement. He had known Dad for years, but had no idea of the wealth my Father possessed. This is what Dad tried to tell me and now I had to figure out why it took 45 years to do so, and then it all fit into place.

Dad never spent anything on himself or showed any wealth, but why? Was Dad an eccentric, I felt not...a loving Father... definitely...a Father who was protecting the one thing he loved more than life itself... Me. Dad was much older than Mother, and while I was growing up Mother often threatened to leave and take me with her, but without any funds she could not leave, so he never revealed to Mother or to anyone. Watching his only daughter become a young adult and act so impetuous, eloping with a stranger who showed no ambition or worthiness added more time for silence. Never could he reveal any wealth to me as he knew the marriage was doomed from the start after meeting the Farrel's. I'm certain that he thought that only a background of poverty would save his precious daughter and granddaughters, as Bob would never have signed away myself or Dad's flesh and blood if he knew there was money but the fact I was poor kindled his will to gladly give me and the girls up without hesitation. Why no help when I was struggling with three small children? Dad had to know that I had grown up and become responsible. He had always been there for love and comfort, but he had to watch me mature into a worth while human being, Why the long wait once I was remarried...he wasn't sure of Ray or of me as yet and until he knew

Ray "a good man" as he told me on our last visit, he could reveal nothing.

Why would Dad not reveal his Jewish background...was it to protect me? Dad saw how often time's Jewish persons are unjustly persecuted and he was trying to protect his own. Many of these questions I hope to find the answers in the months ahead when I delve into the genealogical roots of my family.

What about Mother...how to tell a woman of 65 that she is now a wealthy woman, can have anything she wants. I had to attempt to help her understand why she worked so hard all these years without revealing my deep suspicions. Fortunately Mother didn't seem to ask a lot of questions so my conclusion never had to be explained to her. I just let her think he was eccentric. She did openly remark many times that she couldn't believe that Dad really had anything, but yet she was now set for life with an account at a Brokerage firm who managed her account which I set up so she would receive a sizeable check each month. The home in Eau Claire was completely re-furbished, and Mother continued on in the same life style as she had.

We also spent no more than we had before and only the probate attorney and our immediate family, our daughters knew of our new wealth. I continued to work the same job and purchased nothing until we bought a small vacation condominium in Hilton Head Island, South Carolina.

I now wanted to make money and add to my heritage, squandering nothing and appreciating everything Dad had sacrificed for me. I find, like Dad I too keep a car until it reaches the 200,000 mile mark or it becomes too expensive to operate.

Now I was the one to decide how the fortune was to be invested and what trusts should be set up and I felt totally inept at such a vast undertaking. I had always been the protected one, living hand to mouth and struggling to keep a little home together while working two jobs and supporting three infants. The task was overwhelming and like my Father it became my responsibility solely. I realized I couldn't ask advise from anyone including my husband Ray who could not manage a small law practice, but also needed guidance in his professional work to succeed, so I really trusted no one, and followed very closely the pattern of my Father. I met with the stockbroker Dad used in St. Paul Minnesota and continued the same style of letting dividends roll over, invest in solid long term investments and have been extremely cautious as to using any money.

Mother and I each set up a Trust fund of $10,000.00 for each daughter and I kept it under my control so they would receive it when I felt they were mature enough to handle the money as none at the time appeared capable of handling finances and reminded me of myself as a 20 year old beginning life.

About this time in my life my career took a new path as Montgomery Ward closed their fashion Office and did away with the Wendy Ward program. I was offered either severance pay or the opportunity to go to Wards Interior Design Classes and become the Interior Designer of Montgomery Ward, Randhurst...a large mall in Mount Prospect. I chose the later, as fashions and furnishings go hand in hand and I had a natural talent to combine color, texture, and design. After two years as the interior Designer I decided to stop everything and go back to school and obtain my degree in Interior Design, opening up a new exciting career for me. It was a three-year full-time program at the International Academy of Design located in Chicago adjacent to the Merchandise Mart, and it was not only a wonderful training, but an excellent time to focus on a final career where I could be completely independent and as successful as I had the knowledge and drive to preserver. Graduation from the Academy was witnessed by not only my

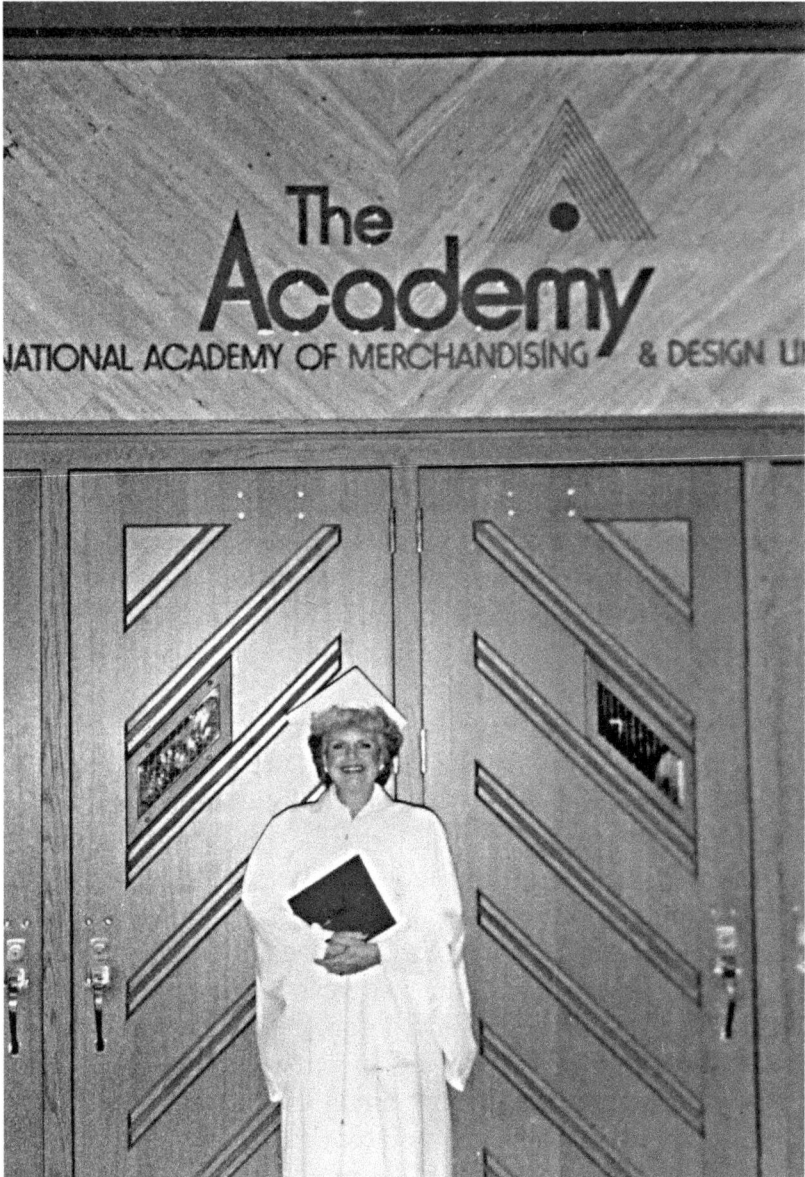

A fresh start

daughters Nancy and Sue but also two grandchildren, Missy and Matt. I was the oldest student among the 75 graduates but non-the-less I received a $500.00 scholarship for most accomplished. The amount was insignificant, but the effort on my part, the dedication and fortitude had paid off and I entered my new career with my own Company established by Ray as a Xmas present, "Jenese Inc." Nancy became the V.P. and Ray the Secretary -treasurer and I was the President and the one doing all the contact work, and overseeing of each job from beginning to end. Beginning anew at a later stage offers many challenges, but the training of my Father, his ability to not only sell the product, but first to sell himself gave me the ground rule to follow. First show the integrity and the dedication to the job with the belief in my ability to do my best and to be the best in my profession. I immediately joined ISID, "International Society of Interior Design" which gave me the credibility needed on my letterhead and business cards. I had a wonderful portfolio of my work from the Design Academy, having shown my ability in design, color, and space planning. How often opportunity is there if only we take the time to stop and evaluate. I did just that in a Kitchen and Bath Showroom, one of the several throughout the Midwest and Florida. I was shopping for kitchen cabinets when I stumbled upon a golden opportunity. I saw display after display being replaced and decorated in the ordinary, non-descript style and so I mentioned it to the manager of the showroom, who was assisting me at the time. As I was voicing my opinion, one of the Company's owners walked into the manager's office. The owner, Harvey Kogan became a personal challenge, a friend, and a critic, all in one. I told him that I felt to spend money and not give a dynamic look that would enhance the cabinets was wrong and I could do much better. A man of few words but great vision, he asked me to be in his office at 8:00 AM the next day with ideas of what I would do. Excited I arrived early and proceeded to stand my design boards with colors and materials set up around his office so he walked into an overwhelming environment. Later I discovered that with Harvey, he calls the shots and this had really taken him back. He asked me what I would charge to do his showrooms and I came in with a very low bid just to get my foot in the door, $25.00, and so began a long rather bumpy relationship, but through it all I totally respected the man who had put his trust and faith in my ideas as I continued to design and decorate his twenty-eight Showrooms. My fee has gone up slightly in the 10 years, but not much only to Harvey I remain on constant call often working under extreme pressure with untimely schedules. I respect his demands and have never let him down, and have done not only his company but also his own residence and that of other members of his family.

I have had hundreds of clients over the twelve years I've had my own Company and each is important to me, many are very difficult, some impossible, but as a Designer I recognize each as a challenge and to date never have had to walk from a job.

Perhaps my most memorable challenge was interviewing for my first Designer Showhouse. In Chicago when a Designer Showhouse is to be shown it is usually a lavish home or one of recognition and the opportunity is opened up to all Designer, a walk thru is scheduled and each Designer brings a portfolio, is interviewed by a panel and it is then that selections are made, usually about 20 designers out of possible 100. It was my first experience, I was a member of ISID and the opportunity to walk thru the "Helen Brach" home was presented to me. Helen Brach was the candy heiress that had mysteriously disappeared nine years before, and presumed murdered; however, to date no body has ever been found and several theories have circled for years. What a challenge for me, a chance to get Jenese Inc. on the map and to become known. My thoughts were racing as I pulled up to the mansion located in Glenview Illinois. Armed with my portfolio which also now included many photos of kitchens and baths that I had designed for KDA, the company in which I had designed many of their Showroom, I entered the foyer, turned in my portfolio and name card, filled out the necessary papers handed to me, and in writing offered to design any portion of the home, even a closet.

After viewing the entire home I returned to the foyer. So many Designers were there, some I had seen before, but no one did I know as this was all so new to me. I only knew that I so wanted to work on the "Helen Brach" home. I was shocked when the panel asked me would I consider the kitchen. The kitchen was very large, in great disarray of water damage to the ceiling over the years, I remembered the kitchen because it reminded me of a giant candy box with red and white stripe ceiling with a ribbon border. I calmly told them I would have to make a telephone call before giving them and answer. I immediately called Harvey Kogan and told him of the opportunity that confronted me, but I needed his help. It was then that an instant friendship formed as he informed me that KDA would give me on loan any appliances, sinks, faucets, or accessories I needed, plus they would custom make and install new counter-tops for the entire kitchen including the island providing they would receive top billing in all publicity that I generated from doing this space. I agreed and informed the committee that I would design the kitchen. From start to finish each Designer has three weeks to complete the space before the press and news media moved in and numerous charity parties are given before the Showhouse opens to the public. Wasting no time I contacted every business I could imagine that could assist me with materials and services, including St. Charles Cabinets, a large upscale manufacturer of kitchen cabinets and which bore the name in the Brach Kitchen. One phone call is all it took and they agreed to refinish all cabinet including new hardware, of which there were over sixty cabinets. A flooring company furnished and installed parquet flooring, Tiffany of Chicago custom designed beautiful lead doors for the cabinets in one area over the built in desk of Helen Brach, as well as a beautiful stained glass window valance on one large picture window. I had people calling me to volunteer goods and services, and I finished putting together a $50,000 kitchen for only $1,000.00 of my money, $500.00, which was for the insurance I had to take out to work on the Showhouse. I was true to my word and KDA was always listed first. The publicity

I received was overwhelming, published in three magazines, newspapers, television where the reporters with their cameramen did their interviewing from the kitchen focusing on the Designer. I had put my heart and soul into this project, went to the library and read the book of Helen Brach's strange disappearance, entitled "Thin Air" and took into consideration, not only the exterior of the home, but also her life-style. The space was designed in "Country French" and the soft cream, apricot and peach glowed with the brass and copper accents, details were everywhere, and accessories included animal artifacts because I had found out that Helen Brach loved animals and supported several animal shelters. Animal canisters and a Save-A-Pet cookbook were on the counter that held her desk, while Bing and Grundel china dogs were set on glass shelves installed in a small window. I received thirty-seven clients from this project, as well as all the publicity and remained in the room everyday for the two weeks it was open to the public to talk of my design and meet the people. This project opened other Showhouses in Chicago to me and I went on to design other kitchens and baths, but they all blur when I think of my first endeavor.

My daughters and Ray don't understand why I continue to work so intensely when financially I have no need, but for my own self-esteem I must feel needed. I enjoy being with people, being creative for each, and hearing their reaction to the final picture, regardless of my financial situation. I enjoy earning money and feeling the euphoria that success brings. A strange notion, not really as I had always been poor when young. We lived modestly and although we had all the necessities, with Mother working shifts in a factory and Dad driving miles in an old panel car to make deliveries to small businesses I always felt necessity to economize so now the feeling of saving and earning one's worth is deeply rooted.

Recognition is great and accomplishments appreciated are so gratifying, so whether it was the many Designer Show Houses I worked on in the Chicago area or possibly an idea I would come up with for some clients problems, I managed to be published as at times the media would contact me to see if I had any new Design idea that they could put in their publications and often I could accommodate. After numerous magazine articles and newspaper publicity I was listed in "Who's Who in Interior Design" in both the national and International Publications with a listing of my accomplishments, of which I was extremely proud as I had worked very hard and developed my company on my own.

Two years after my Father's death my Mother became very ill and was diagnosed with cancer of the cervix and of the lungs. I left for Eau Claire immediately and spent the next six to eight weeks getting Mother thru a crisis period. Her fear and depression was threatening to worsen the outcome of her surgeries and radiation treatments so I had to convince her to eat, be optimistic and have strength in order to undergo such drastic treatments. I had to remain strong and it did take all my strength to put on a "happy face" and encourage her, but I kept telling myself, that "I am a Tuffie". I only cried when I would retreat after I left her side and went to the hospital chapel or back to our home in Eau Claire. Mother did recover from her two surgeries and radiation with a favorable prognosis. All of the cancer had been removed and she only had to return to the Eau Claire clinic every six months for check-ups. The doctor did suggest that she should move near family, and since I was all the family there was, she agreed to move to Mount Prospect, but wanted a place of her own, so at last I was able to get her a home with a view. Ray and I found a beautiful Condominium in Mt. Prospect on a golf course with a deck overlooking a duck pond. Her unit was a spacious two bedroom, living room with dining room extension, wonderful kitchen with separate eating area and sliding doors to her balcony. I proceeded to completely refurbish it to a beautiful sophisticated interior complete with beveled mirror walls at the end of the dining room and silk Moiré wall-covering to match her beautiful moiré draperies in the living room, over elegant French Terrell sheers. All colors were in the soft "Champagne" tone and even the closets were edged in tapestry, while her bedroom had an elegant finely pleated bed covers with bed skirt and draperies and sheers to match. Nothing was too good for my Mother as she was now a wealthy woman starting a new life and could be what ever she wanted to be and even take on a whole new image. Her furniture was all in Henderon Cherry and oil paintings highlighted with crystal accented her lighting. Her only furniture we moved from Eau Claire was her bedroom set and her living-room console television. I was attempting to give her all she deserved after so many years of going without. The final touch was an elegant fountain on her deck and planters filled with petunias and pansies added a colorful homey touch. New comfy chairs and tables finished the deck area. I had moved all of the clothes and personal belongings and I did all this in three weeks while Mother was in the hospital. I really was proud of my accomplishment, but I always amaze myself with what I can accomplish when under pressure. Debby flew to Eau Claire to drive Mother down along with her cat, Tashia. I'll never forget Mother's face when I opened her condominium door, the music played in the background her favorite piece, "Dear Heart" and the coffee and coffee cake were all ready. She was like a stunned, timid child, a school-girl unable to speak with eyes wide open and tears streaming down her face, and I knew all of my efforts had been completely successful. She finally had her beautiful home with a gorgeous view, and so quiet.

Never did Mother change anything in the twelve years she lived there as she would state, "Why change a beautiful dream," and so she became the person I knew she always wanted to be, but never had the opportunity to do so before. She had her hair done weekly had regular manicures and became very active and popular in the Senior Center as she weekly took coffeecakes and sweet rolls for the entire Center. It was her way of sharing what she had as she said many lived on pensions. She was now a matron of means and loved her new role, never really questioning, but sometimes she would tell me that she still couldn't believe that she had any money, even when she would get her monthly check from the Investment house. One occasion I took Mother into a Buick agency and bought her the taupe Buick in the window of the showroom. She had always had a Chevrolet that she had paid for herself, a stripped down model, the most economical for getting to work and errands. She couldn't believe we were shopping for a luxury car for her, but when she saw the one in the window, I could see sparkle in he eyes and I knew it had to be hers.

Her only real extravaganzas were on her four grand-daughters as she so wanted to give them each a car for college graduation, starting with Susan, Debby, and Darcy, and six years later for Nancy. Her generosity with the girls gave her more enjoyments from life than any other part of her life. Life before her move to Mount Prospect and before Dad died had been of hard work and many lonely hours when she was alone. How sad that she and Dad had money to enjoy together and yet Dad couldn't risk losing his daughter, so he shared nothing with Mother. How sad that these two wonderful people could not be molded together to make a strong bond. Mother knew so little about Dad, not his real name, his birth year, his real age, or anything about his heritage, and it always amazes me that none of these questions ever surfaced in the 45 years of their marriage.

Now that Mother was all set and comfortable and my company was established Ray and I decided to take a do-it yourself tour of Ireland and Scotland for a much needed R & R. Ray planned the entire trip, made all the reservations for accommodations and we began our two week jaunt with a stop at Ashford Castle, a magnificent castle located in northern Ireland, where the filming of "The quiet Man" starring John Wayne and Maureen O'Hara had taken place. The course was spectacular and never have I shot such a round of golf as it was manicured to perfection. Staying at my first castle with all the amenities was also very exciting. Our real introduction to golf in Ireland and Scotland came with our next course. Ballybunion where the thickets of Heather were impossible and the bunkers required a ladder to enter. After one round of gold and forty-eight lost balls between the two of us in two days, we decided that we really didn't know how to play golf after all. The caddies tried but were also unable to find our balls, and I had to aim for goat trails as the greens were beyond my reach and between the drive and the green was only the rough up to my knees. From Ballybunion we played Troon and Prestwick we went on to Turnberry where we also planned to stay for two days. We never got to Glen Eagle or St. Andrew's as we got a call during the night fiom Aunt Ruth, my sister in law that said Mother had been in a tragic car accident and was in the hospital in critical condition. The management at Turnberry made all the arrangements and soon we were on the next flight out of Shannon and on our way back to Chicago. I now was no longer the "Tuffie" for I was numb...I had left Mother so happy and apparently also healthy and here she was now fighting for her life. I had lost my Father without being able to say, "I love and to be there, and now I was praying that God would let me see Mother before taking her from me. My prayers were answered as Mother did linger for five months, but the Doctor had told me that 85% of her heart muscle had been destroyed by a severe heart attack in the Emergency room and there was no way she could live. She had been hit broad-side by a 20 year old rough character who had rebuilt an old pickup with oversized tires and went thru the stop light at the corner where Mother lived. She was making a turn when he went thru and hit her. After the accident, with Mother semi-conscious and in pain he stood in front of her car hitting his fists on her hood using profanity. He was ticketed, but had no insurance, or knowledge that his profound brutal attack toward my Mother, in my opinion caused her to have the heart attack and cost her life. She was never without oxygen again and daily she became weaker and weaker. I kept the truth from her and moved in with her to give her constant care and support, but, she didn't want to feel she was disrupting my life, still thinking Jenese first, and wanted me to hire someone so I could live at home, about five miles from her. I called a very dear friend, a private-duty nurse, and a girl Mother had known since she was twelve years old, Donna Rikansrud, better known as Ricky. She lived about 90 miles away in Wisconsin, and she drove down immediately and became Mothers live in friend and nurse for the 4½ remaining months from Monday thru Friday, and I moved in on weekends. I also ate evening meals with Mother and Ricky and often Ray would join us, after dinners for a game of Cuba, some conversation and then off to bed for Mother. She got up and dressed everyday still wearing lace hankies in her pocket and her hair always combed and make-up on. Always a lady, although she would ask me form time to time why wasn't she getting better, but felt so weak, and I would tell her it takes a long time to mend a damaged heart. After I left her I cried all the way home, often cried myself to sleep, knowing the inevitable, but yet I thanked God I had this cherished time with her. A week before she died I told her the truth as she knew and wanted me to look into her eyes and tell her the truth. It gave her time to talk about Dad, the girls, her concerns for each and would they squander the trust we had set up for each. I assured her that I would give the money when they were old enough to use it wisely and that I would also see each would get what ever she wanted to give them. She talked about each granddaughter with such love and depth, as I had never heard her insight into their personalities before. She believed Debby was the most like me, she seemed so full of life and happy with a gift for writing that she attributed to Dad. She saw Darcy as a loving, caring sensitive girl, so dependent and most like her, facing each day with uncertainties, but always putting on a brave face. Sue, she though was the most ambitious and family oriented. That she would always protect her family and she believed she had a challenging future with her in-laws, but her love of family and her strength would see her thru. Nancy was the brightest of the four, and perhaps the strongest and the most dependable for me as location would so determine. Her last concern was for her beloved cat, Tashia, a stray, older cat that thru Mother had learned to sleep on satin with Mother, drink half-in-half, and sleep in the sun on Mother's deck, listening only to soft music. Nancy promised to take Tashia as Mother was concerned as we had dogs and Nancy was a single gal living in a high-rise in Chicago, having just graduated from law School. Nancy did take Tashia and kept her for 10 years when she died almost reaching the age of twenty. Every evening when I left Mother's Condominium I didn't know if she would ever be there tomorrow, and on March 16th, Ricky called and said Mother had slipped away in her sleep, quiet and peaceful. I truly now felt like and orphan, the first time in my life I ever felt alone, and yet I had Ray and the four girls, but Mother had been like my best friend for 12 years and now she was gone and I had never felt so lost. Another small service was held at he Methodist church and the same minister, Larry Hinkleman presided, but this time I wrote the Epitaph for her grave marker which reads...

> A soul so great and yet so small
> Who's love of life captured all.
> The roles in life she took in stride...
> With courage and a sense of pride...
> But falter not to the end...
> She gave her love, my special friend.
> My Mother

Mother is buried next to Dad and now I have increased the plot to cover six graves and have also had a granite bench placed where I can sit and meditate and talk to Mother and Dad. I have Dad's famous writing on side in a relief pattern and signed Israel David Mondschine and on the other side, the name of Busch. It's such a peaceful place, but it still is difficult for me to go visit, which I always do alone, but once there I do get a sense of peace.

Mother's death was very difficult for me to accept, as she seemed so alive and vital, having overcome cancer, Dad's death and finally was enjoying her golden years when an accident caused by some non-caring person ended it all. I felt that I needed a spiritual uplifting, I needed a sign or a need to reach out to God, and so my thought now turned to Tibet, which is the highest altitude for anyone to go to on this Earth. I had never really been openly religious, never openly expressed my faith, life had always been good to Jenese, but now for the first time I felt the need to communicate with God.

Tibet is the rooftop of the world and it became my obsession to seek an answer to my great loss in this far away place, and yet never before had I even thought of such a region to visit. Entering Tibet is no easy feat as the borders are seldom open to foreigners but following Tiananmen Square with tourism dropping off in China, the borders were opened and we left immediately for Tibet. Our route took in a tour of that part of the world starting with India, Pakistan, Nepal and ending in Tibet. Our trip not only filled my needs but also offered one of our most unusual itineraries ever ventured by us. India was eye-opening as never before had we witnessed such poverty and suffering and my burden seemed to lessen by just seeing living souls surviving in squalor and filth, small children starved with bloated abdomens. The world needs many more Mother Theresa's to grant dignity to such stricken people. Never before had I stepped over bodies lying in the street waiting to be picked up by a wooden truck and taken to the cremation site where ashes are then dumped into the Ganges. How my heart ached for these poor untouchable humans. One soul I did reach out to and I'll never forget her, as she was one of the pathetic, a middle-aged woman cleaning the bathrooms at the airport. She was barefoot and in rags and how the words of my Father's famous lines rang in my ears... "I wept because I had no shoes, and then I saw a man who had no feet." Our eyes meet and she looked down with the sadness of a child crying on the inside, but silent on the outside. I reached into my purse and handed her a gardenia sachet I had been carrying to help mask the stench of India. I also gave her a few gadgets from my purse, which she took and looked astonished that I would give her these items, which she held very close to her heart. I then took an extra Visa picture of myself I carried and gave it to her along with some Indian coins. She kissed my picture and the corners of her mouth turned upward. When I left the restroom I was in tears and turning to leave the airport later I saw her standing in the doorway holding my picture to her heart.

On the other side of the coin was the owner of a marble factory in Agra. After visiting the Taj Mahal that was indescribably magnificent we stepped thru the gates where on the exterior people were dying of starvation. Children were begging for food, many of them without the lower portion of their arms as they had been amputated so they could be more appealing to foreigners as they begged. This was told to us on the tour and it is impossible to fathom such inhumane cruelty; however, our tour guide also stated that the only hope for India was a massive extermination of its lower cast...another unbelievable statement that I shall never forget, and for the remainder of the trip I couldn't look or speak to this cruel individual. When we entered the Marble factory where outside starving people leaned against the exterior was parked a new Mercedes. The owner an elegantly dressed man wearing several gold chains greeted us. He asked me how I liked India and I commented that while I marveled at the beauty of the Taj Mahal I also told him that I couldn't get past the suffering and poverty of the people. His response was one I'll never forget as he said, "What poverty and suffering...we are all well off in India," and his attitude and statement sickened me. Never do I wish to return to India and I pray that someway the suffering of its people shall someday end.

Pakistan is Muslim, but there seems to be no begging, the parts of Lahore that we visited seemed clean and beautiful and the people seem proud of their heritage. While visiting the Red Fort I spoke to one of the guards and mentioned how beautiful I found Lahore. The next thing I knew he asked if I'd like to come to his home in the evening for dinner. Naturally I had to decline, and set off to find Ray who had wandered off to take photos. This usually happens on all trips and it's a miracle that we never loose each other, but somehow sooner or later we meet. No sooner had I caught up to Ray than the guard came running with his supervisor again to make the sincere offer. What better way to see the culture and meet the people than in one's home and so we accepted. Again it was one of the highlights of tour trip and like the others I tend to reach out, to seek new ideas and explore. This I inherit from my Father who would always talk to strangers and went out of his way for ones less fortunate. The guard turned out to be the Assistant Superintendent of Prisons and was considered well-to-do in Pakistan. He had his own car and driver and a very nice home located behind a walled complex, which he shared with his brothers and their wives as well as his Mother. I asked him if his wife was concerned about his bringing strangers home even though we had no intention of eating, but only to visit. He answered that he hadn't informed her but then he said why would she mind. This was the very first time he had ever done it, as I was the first foreigner to ever speak to him. Needless to say his wife was stunned when we walked in as she was dressed in a simple housedress and the two small children, a boy 5 and a girl 7 were in their play clothes. Our host immediately asked us to sit down in the living room while he ran to his brothers and Mother's home to invite them to meet us. All came and all were dressed in their finery with gold chains and silk Sari's, all except his wife who never changed her expression all evening and looked like she was in shock. We found out so much about their customs that evening and while all five brothers spoke English very well and had Government jobs, the wives and Mother spoke no English and only

165

smiled and nodded. The Mother is revered and all catered to her, especially her daughter-in-laws, as she had chosen each for her sons. She also had daughters of her own and as is the custom, the daughters get married first and the males of the family all work for dowries to pay for their sister's marriage and then Mama starts choosing wives for the eldest son first and on down. When I asked what if the son didn't like the girl his Mama chose, the men asked why wouldn't they, as their Mother knew what was best for them. The divorce rate in Pakistan must not exist. The family was delightful and we watched movies of the wedding of our Host and also birthday parties of his son where they hire a band, decorate profusely and have 100 guests, but there is no celebration for the daughter's birthday at all. What an experience we had in a part of the world so foreign to us. From Pakistan it was on to Katmandu, Nepal and again a beautiful part of the world. The city is full of shrines and Mosques and is clean and lovely. The children seem happy and people are working and appear contented. We did witness the "Living Goddess" behind a curtained window in her palace. She was a young girl of eight who looked like a miniature adult as the balcony windows opened and she appeared on the curtain-draped balcony for her public audience. She appears once a week for short view; otherwise is always behind closed windows and doors as she's considered a Goddess, a chosen perfect child without a blemish and remains in seclusion until the age of puberty when she is released to her parents who are paid handsomely for their young daughter, possibly as an infant. People actually worship this girl much like the Dali Lhama of Tibet. She can be visited once a month by her parents, but otherwise is kept her entire developmental life in seclusion. Once released they never marry or really ever fit into society, as was pointed out to us. As she stood on the balcony she appeared like a beautiful marble statue, fully made up with heavy make-up and ornamental dress and jewels and was adorned like a royal princess, but never did she glance at the people but only looked out into space as in a trance.

At last our final leg of the trip was upon us and we arrived in Lhasa, Tibet after flying over the Himalayan Mts. and seeing Mount Everest in all its glory. It's awesome to know that you are viewing he highest place on our planet Earth and it is a humbling experience. Tibet was my destination and my destiny and there is where I was looking for that mystical answer that I needed, a sign of hope that once again I would see my beloved Mother and Father and they could touch me in some mystical way to help me understand and believe, I knew I had always believed in God and had never really questioned, but now I did have questions and needed some outward sign. I only prayed that something would touch my heart and give me hope and an ongoing faith.

When we arrived in Lhasa we were told to go to our room and retire immediately and take oxygen for at least one hour. When we arrived at our hotel, the Holiday Inn, I was surprised to see a familiar name in such a remote area. We found out later that it is the only westernized hotel in all of Tibet, and that only the manager, who lived on the premises, spoke English. Since we only had one week in Tibet I chose not to waste that precious hour by going to bed and taking oxygen, as I didn't need such a treatment and so I encouraged Ray to join me in a rickshaw ride instead to see this fabulous city. A short time later we returned to the hotel, as I was experiencing one of the most severe headaches I had ever had, and nausea and vomiting soon followed. The air sickness or lack of oxygen landed me in bed for 24 hours and because of my illness we had to remain behind in Lhasa for the week while the rest of the tour left the next morning for remote parts of Tibet. The manager served me a huge bowl of noodles and broth and within 24 hours I was up and ready to spend one of the most memorable weeks of my life. Fate must have had a hand in keeping us behind, as this is where I was to find my sign. Ray and I covered the usual tourist attractions, which includes a visit to Potala, the home of the Dali Lhama and realized immediately the love the people of Tibet have for their religious leader. Everywhere we went Tibetans would ask us if we had a picture of Dali Lhama as all pictures of their great leader are banned in Tibet and they don't even know what he looks like. That is the only English they speak, and how I wish I had taken many photos with me, but no doubt the Chinese would have punished the people if they found the photos. We wandered all around Lhasa, going to forbidden places and because we were just the two of us my feelings are that is why we were never stopped, but a tour would have been turned away.

The Tibetans were curious, friendly, and often just smiled their broad smiles as I attempted to try on their traditional hats or spin their wonderful prayer wheels. Everyplace we went we saw Yaks as the Yaks are their beasts of burden and are used for fuel for fires, by way of Yak Dung. They use yak oil to light there candles in the monasteries using Yak oil, and also as a source of food, and clothing. They respect and take great care of their animals and I saw the peasants feeding their Yaks and cows bananas and other foods. Our scheduled tour in Lhasa did not include the Deprong Monastery on the outskirts of Lhasa and one that is reached only on foot as there is no road up the mountain. It is the highest spot in all of Tibet where one can be unless it is perhaps somewhere on the Himalayan peaks themselves, and it was there that I had the urge to go. We took two rickshaws to where the dirt road ended and looked straight upwards at the monastery perched on top. We saw monks dressed in their golden robes scaling up and down the mountain, including seven-year-old monks. And so I convinced Ray that we could also make the trek and asked our Rickshaw riders to wait for us. The climb didn't seem so endless until we began, and with the steep slope of the path and the thinness of the air at such a high altitude I was starting to wonder if in fact we would ever reach the top. We were both exhausted, hanging onto tree limbs and yet continuing on as I seemed to be driven to reach the top, not knowing what I'd find. After what seemed like hours we reached the monastery only to find that it is not open to outsiders; however, the monks had been watching us struggle to

Lhasa, Tibet Shopping in Tibetan market

Lhasa, Tibet, Duprong, Monastery
Signs of immortality appeared to me

reach the top and opened their gigantic carved doors to us and beckoned us inside with gestures. Once inside we saw a two story prayer wheel which the monks spin both entering and leaving, and we also saw monks of all ages, including very small boys (age seven) as we found out that is when they can enter the monastery studying and praying for a better tomorrow. Their chant with the prayer wheel is "Amee...Amee...Aman", which is the version we heard...such beautiful passive people. As we stood inside the doors of Deprung we saw 50 or more narrow steps going almost straight up which we climbed with extreme difficulty as I still was filled with the need to get to the highest spot. The weather was clear, sunny with no hint of rain and yet when we reached the top and looked out at the view we saw the most beautiful rainbow I had ever seen. Call it coincidence, but to me it was the sought after sign I longed for. Ray too was speechless as we stood in silence observing this beautiful heavenly vision, not seen from below. My spirits almost lifted as I felt an inspirational experience never before felt and I knew all the effort and waiting was answered and I should now find peace of mind. I needed what God told me that a promise of tomorrow awaited and all was beautiful and I should go on knowing peace and love, for Mother was now with Dad and both were watching over me. We left DePrung sometime later and received yet another sign of assurance as behind my rickshaw when we reached the bottom of the mountain was a small Pomeranian dog that looked exactly like my parents dog, "Pixie". Where he came from no one knew, but all of the other dogs of Tibet that I had seen had a much different look and we had seen hundreds but never a Pomeranian. The little dog started to run after my Rickshaw and even though we kept stopping and I offered him food and water, he stepped back and remained out of reach, but would take up the task of running after me as we rode into Lhasa. He did so all the way to the Holiday Inn where the dog stopped and watched me. Then turned and left. Ray and I were so stunned and Ray told me that it looked exactly like Mother & Dad's dog and that all was right and I should be at peace. We never saw the dog again, nor did I ever see another Pomeranian again while we were in Tibet or until we reached America. This is without a doubt the strangest phenomenon that has ever happened to me, and so I left Tibet with peace of mind and now the veil of wonderment and confusion has been lifted.

Since that trip we have continued to travel to unseen places, by cruise ships, tours, trains and on our own, including our wonderful month tour of New Zealand, touring New Zealand by cruise ship and flying to Australia to meet some dear friends we had met in Chicago years before, Lillian and Ralph Schubert. Hosted by these lovely people, we saw Sydney from the hilltop as they live in French's Cove overlooking the city. We stood outside looking at the millions of lights flickering below, while she had the music of Frank Sinatra's, "Chicago, Chicago" on the record player. We danced, had a wonderful home-style dinner and bid our Aussie friends good-bye as we left via plane for the Outback. The Outback and Alice Springs was very exciting to me as I love the more unusual, different cultures and unique people, and the Aborigine are just that. We walked around the base of Ayers Rock at sunrise, and I climbed up into one of the caves while Ray took my picture...that was before the tour began at 9:00 a.m. and we were told we could not get within 100 yards of the holy rock...we had left our sunrise viewers and ventured off alone so were unaware of the regulations, but no harm was done as no one knew, only we knew and according to solitude at sunrise and the low climbing of the rock really uplifted my spirits and although I wanted to share this marvelous experience with our tour companions, we kept it our secret. I broke another barrier as I managed to feed and give water to a Dingo, a wild dog, so thin and forlorn looking on in the distance as a group of over 100 shared a candle light barbecue at Ayers Rock. I went off into the shadows with two rather large bowls, which I found empty, filling one with water and the other with meat. Again no one saw me, except Ray was rather concerned as he tried to mingle and draw any attention away from me. This is something I'm certain my Father would have done as well, as wherever we travel I take extra food from the restaurant, the cruise ship, or I buy some food at local food stores to feed the strays, of which there are many. My favorite portion of the entire trip was when we left the tour and went on alone to the Great Barrier Reef. I cannot imagine going so far and missing one of the most spectacular sights in the world and one of the natural wonders of the earth. We flew to Carnes and drove by autobus to Port Douglas, which is one of the great excursion areas into the Reef. We boarded the "Quicksilver", a small vessel with approx. 200 persons aboard and left for the Continental shelf. There we anchored and we were given equipment to either snorkel or scuba dive. I never actually learned to swim, only float, and I had one attempt to snorkel. I had been shown how by my son-in-law, Mike on one of our Caribbean cruises, but it was off shore and not in this vast environment. A pontoon was tied to the ship and from there each passenger would slide into the water, there were buoys anchored to form a very large area for snorkeling, to see the marvels below. I explained to one of the life guards, of which there were several, that I couldn't swim, but he informed me that with my life jacket, fins and gear as well as the salt water, I would have a difficult time to sink, non the less I slid into the tepid clear water and hung onto the very large rope tied between the buoys. Soon I found myself mesmerized and just floating around, snorkeling as a professional, and enjoying the greatest show on earth. The colors of the corals were unbelievable, and the creatures were breath taking, I had no idea of the beauty that lies beneath the sea, and the multitude of wild life and although we bought tapes of the Barrier Reef and Ray took underwater pictures of the Reef, only the actual experience of seeing it can give the true images. How I wished I could have been one of the Scuba divers actually walking among, or swimming among that beauty, but I was thrilled we had snorkeled in the Reef when we did. We repeated the snorkeling the next day off one of the many small Islands that dot the Reef and we tendered out to the Island where many thatched umbrellas dotted the beach. Under my umbrellas was a large piece of coral lying in the sand, which I managed to take with me when I left. This tiny piece of the coral Reef I treasure, and hopefully I broke no law as it was not attached to anything and looked like it needed a special home. It is now in a special cabinet with other artifacts from Australia and New Zealand.

Our last trip taken also had deep meaning to me as one ages the need for complete spiritual conviction seems more important and so our trip to the Holy Land was very special and although there were terrorist attacks we had none the time we were there.

We began our three week tour on a Cruise to the Holy Land by flying direct to Istanbul on our own four days ahead of the tour itself so we would have the chance to not only see this marvelous city spanning two continents, but would have time to mingle and feel the culture before boarding the Cruise ship, where time is so structured. We obtained a room across from Hagia Sophia, the oldest Mosque in Istanbul, and very centrally located. Our room at St. Sophia was in an old monastery, several centuries old with very thick walls, and 12' ceilings, and reasonably priced, as it had no air conditioning. I prefer such lodging as the charm and beauty was there and the coolness of this old monastery with its inner courtyard serving lovely breakfast included to its guests was outstanding...and all for $79.00 per night...whereas other luxurious hotels were anywhere from $300.00 per night and up. When traveling we usually shop around and look for authenticity, charm and of course price. We would awaken every morning with the wailing calls to worship and hear the call throughout Istanbul with all the mosques. We were there during Princess Diana's death and our small black and white TV carried little else.

Our first night after a succulent dinner in one of the Cisterns under the street of Istanbul we were awakened in the middle of the night by a call from our daughter Nancy. She was so excited as she said, "Mother the old log home next door to us in Barrington Hills has been repossessed by the bank and is going on public auction tomorrow, and we could be neighbors." She went on and on with, "You and Dad aren't getting any younger and we could watch the home when you travel, and you could watch the children grow." There were three very small children, Frankie age 5, Jack David age 2 and Danielle age 1. After three calls during the night I finally told her that I would talk it over with Dad over a 6:00 a.m. breakfast and call her back. Reasoning with an ultra conservative husband who has been awakened three times during the night, and one who is extremely slow moving is not an easy task, but several things came into play, all attributed to my Father's keen teaching. First I have the ability to convince within reason, and it was true, we weren't getting any younger, we no longer were close to any of our neighbors in Mount Prospect, as all of our close friends had moved long ago. But the main reason was that we could watch the grandchildren grow and be next to our wonderful Nancy, and if anything happened to either of us we would have family next door. Another factor was that I did control solely my inheritance and could do as I so wished, but nevertheless harmony in marriage is important. Naturally Ray objected and naturally I called Nancy and told her to bid on the land only, 5 acres, which is the code in Barrington Hills as it is horse country and many own stables. Nancy and Franco own 11 acres and I had purchased the adjoining 5 acres of ravine and set it a land trust for the three children to keep their investment private and the children safe. Property in Barrington Hills is expensive so when I told her to bid on land only she said she thought we'd never get it, but after a hectic day of sight seeing when Ray totally never saw anything he looked at, but only a disastrous situation ahead. In a way he was correct as when we returned to St. Sophia a telegram awaited with only two words, "welcome neighbors"...and we knew. From then on Ray's vacation was ruined, but I proceeded with sheer joy at the prospect that awaited us, as well as the wonders of seeing Jerusalem, Bethlehem, and reliving the pages of the Bible.

We walked the 12 stages that Jesus walked before he was crucified...we visited Nazareth where Jesus spoke in the temple and stayed with Paul and I knelt and kissed the spot where Christ was born in Bethlehem 2000 years ago. After our visit I felt reconfirmed that Christ was the Savior and I would see Mother and Dad again, and although life on earth is beautiful if you just make it so, that life is also beyond with a serene beauty that only comes when you leave this earth.

Close to Nature

Winter in the country

The log home is soon to be our permanent home and I have spent the past two years rehabbing a total disaster, as the previous owner who supposedly was an eccentric not only left during the night after three years of non payment of taxes or other services, but also took a large pot belly stove from the main room, leaving a huge hole in the floor and a hanging chimney sending soot over the entire area. Plumbing was either broken or removed and light fixtures were missing, only wires remained. All in all even I with my trained eye at first had to catch myself as we viewed the home, and Ray was near having a coronary. I did however, see large old worm wood beams separating two areas, and from that built a fabulous country kitchen complete with "Chicago bricks" chopped in half length wise by Ray, 190 bricks which I had installed on the kitchen walls bringing a look of authenticity "Blue Bahia" granite tops the counters of custom cabinets hand made in England, and designed by me as to shape, height, and all details. All turned out as I had envisioned and the home which is now close to 3,000 sq. ft. from an original 1,300 sq. ft home is unique. Mike, Sue's husband said, "It's no log cabin, but a log castle." The small screened in porch with crumbling cement and tom screens gave way to a magnificent 23 ft. x 32 ft. great room with 22 ft. ceiling. The ceilings throughout the entire home are pine, and I blended all colors and oversaw all work, likewise the pine floors. The great room was designed around a gigantic gothic transom well over 100 years old which flanked the entrance to the Chemistry Lab at the University of Chicago where I had worked on several dormitories as a Designer. At the time I went to the head of Building and grounds and asked if I could have some of the classroom doors and the two transoms in lieu of any design fee to be charged the University. He agreed and after years of storage these two beautiful transoms now are set within pine. One is in the great room where the sun streams thru the diamond panes at sunset, and the other is set in the master bedroom ceiling, sloping to 15 ft. to enhance this marvelous transom. The fireplace at the end of the great room is no doubt the focal pint of the log home as the stones, very muted in color take on the look, with their large sizes, irregular shapes and flat surface reminding me of an old castle, and with the proper lighting it truly is awesome. The mantel is a cedar tree, which was high in a barn in Peshtigo, Wisconsin. I had heard about the barn, one of two structures that were left standing after the Peshtigo fire of 1860. I also heard that the two structures were being dismantled, so we drove to Peshtigo and I climbed up into a high loft, marked this 26 ft. Cedar tree with a tube of lipstick and had a mantel cut from it. We were present for the cutting of the log to give a level surface, as well as the back of the tree so it could be anchored and set into the stone. All had to be coordinated perfectly, but in all my years I now realize I am a perfectionist, a Virgo, and sometimes I drive myself crazy with minor details, but I always get things done and 99% of the time I am pleased with

A deer completes the picture

the outcome. I not only love detail, but also do so enjoy being creative.

The home is now done, including a two story cat room complete with spiral staircase for the cats to go from their furnished eating area and litter-box area (two rooms), to their upper level which is all in stained logs, and pine ledges on which to sit and watch the birds and Deer. Nothing is too good for our beloved stray animals. The dogs have a very large fenced area and have their own room, both heated and air-conditioned, complete with a laundry room (Nancy's idea) and cabinetry for their supplies. They run in and out of their doggie door and love their new space.

Even the wild life have a spot on a our five acres as I had an old oval bath-tub sunk edging the wooded area, have an aerator in the bottom of the tub to keep the water moving and a heater floating on top to keep the water from freezing. Debby has sent bird and deer feeders, which are set in their place and St. Frances of Assisi which Darcy, bought for us, oversees all. Salt licks and troughs of deer food should attract the deer while nearby eight birdhouses and stands filled for birds and squirrels should also help the wild life thru the harsh winters in Illinois.

Were the expenditures foolish...I think not as it is a prime land investment and should not decrease in value, but increase as land in this area always seems to be sought after, so to justify my other reasons for being impetuous in buying a home site unseen, I also counter it with the idea of the expenditure of being a saving investment.

All of the properties I now own, the log home, my parents home in Eau Claire, Wisconsin, my Mother's condominium in Mt. Prospect, Illinois and our three properties in Hilton Head Island including our great home on deep water I now see as investments the stock market fluctuates but land investment seems to be rather steady. I never thought too much about what to buy or sell before recently when a trip for my yearly check-up revealed, something new and foreign to me. I had enlarged lymph glands, which didn't seem to bother, but after a biopsy, it was revealed that I had Chronic Lymphoma...the doctor said I probably will die with it, and not because of it, and estimated that I had carried this slow developing lymphoma in my system for 10 years or more.

The sounds of lymphoma, a cancer of the lymph glands at first was rather terrifying to me and to my family, but I am really not worried. I have known nothing but excellent health my whole life, and what a full and wonderful life I have had...Energy is still mine and although sometimes I push more than I used to in order to fill goals I set for myself, I now take a somewhat different perspective on the uncertain future. I now have written and re-written my will two or three times, changing it as grandchildren are added and to date there are ten, including the youngest Joseph Jeneson Laterza, named after me for a middle name a precious little baby of six weeks with bright, clear eyes and I wonder if I shall watch him play soccer as I have the others or excel in piano as they have done...but then life is unsure and so I live each day to the fullest and never put off till tomorrow what I can do today. I, unlike my Father have to give some of my wealth to family before estate taxes take so much, but now with George W. Bush as President, I do hope he will thru the Republican agenda do away with the estate tax, and help people that have saved a lifetime so they can pass their wealth onto family. Each year I manage to give a portion of the estate to the grandchildren and have plans to even do more if time permits.

My quest for the truth and the exploring of Genealogical records has uncovered so much that I would have never known, and answers many questions that have haunted me. One fact that I uncovered is that my Father had an Uncle William Mondschine who had been in business with my Grandfather David Mondschine in Arkansas. They had land holdings together and at the time of Grand-father's death at the age of 39, my uncle cheated David's widow, Fannie Mondschine out of her due right to the land, and kept everything for himself. This no doubt also played a role in my

Father's mistrust of his fellow man, and so my Father kept his secrets sharing with no one. He almost lived a life of solitude and silence, yet he so loved to converse with anyone on many subjects, but never his private life, waiting for his daughter to mature into a trusting adult that he could share his life with. I also found that his grand-father, Fannie's Father, Levi Rosenblatt was a Jewish Rabbi and therefore to have my Father leave temple was very difficult. His brother-in-law cheated my Father out of money, when my Father worked and pinched pennies, but gave to family, a loan which never was repaid.

As for Mother, her saga is even more severe. All the stories I've been told as a child were only in fact partial truths as her life had taken a tragic twist as a young girl. It's true she was left without a Father at young age, but not thru death. Her Father, my grand-father abandoned his family of seven children and left for Alaska to find his fortune and never returned. Years later he was found in California but disappeared again, but I shall track Louis Platte thru research and find the truth and date of his death if possible. When my Mother was eight years old, and it was believed her Father was dead, my Grandmother married again, a judge, who not only bedded his wife, but my Aunt Orliene, age 10 and possibly my Mother, but that was never confirmed. After the sexual attacks on the little girls, my Grandmother divorced him and in order not to have a scandal, his family paid off my Grandmother not to press charges. What heartache and scandal for the time was 1916 and not only was divorce a disgrace, but sexual abuse was an abomination...never to be discussed openly. To place Mother and Orliene out of reach and harms way from this tragedy my Grandmother placed the children in a children's home, to be nurtured by the nuns. Their time spent there was more of repression of feelings and keeping everything a deep dark secret. No wonder sex was never discussed in our home, and even the normal maturing and experiencing menstruation was so traumatic to me. The shyness...the repression...the never asking, always accepting whatever life gives, the fear of men, all men, led my

Mother to the state that I knew and remembered. No doubt my Father was just that to her…a Father figure, one to never question, but also never to really be close to as he was a man, and so these two lonely denied people lived entire lives for one purpose…namely me.

Much of the above information was received not from the Archives nor from family history, but from my elderly Aunt Agnes, the wife of my only living relative on Mother's side, her younger bother, Robert. Agnes told me of the half-brother incident, of my Mother and aunt's horrible experience and the scared memories of the family. My uncle Robert is reluctant to talk about anything and almost in denial and is unwilling to let me pursue more of the family history with Agnes, but at least thru her information and courage I have unveiled much of my Mother's life and for that I am very grateful.

The future I find the days filled with life and contentment, with the knowledge that I can watch over my family. I can live a wonderful life, enjoy all the amenities that someone with means can enjoy, always appreciative of the sacrifice and love, the humility and scrutinizing, the careful planning and ever patience that prevailed throughout my Father's life. I too shall make mistakes along the way and at present feel animosity for one of my grandchildren that has hurt her Mother, but hopefully that will change soon. Nothing worldly could bring me the pleasure as such as seeing my entire family together, sharing happy times and yet with each daughter there is a new life and a new challenge that might not fit into my greater plan; and so I shall attempt to show the wisdom and patience of one who waits and prays to the Almighty for Guidance, for I am MY FATHER'S DAUGHTER.

Ended November 23, 2002
(My Mother's Birthday)

www.ingramcontent.com/pod-product-compliance
Lightning Source LLC
Chambersburg PA
CBHW021059090426

42738CB00006B/424